BETTER BY THE DOZEN, PLUS TWO:

ANECDOTES AND A PHILOSOPHY OF LIFE FROM A FAMILY OF SIXTEEN

By James and Kathleen Littleton

Copyright © 2007 by James & Kathleen Littleton
First Edition

All rights reserved to authors. No part of this book shall be reproduced, stored in a retrieval system, or transmitted by any means without written permission from the author.

All scripture excerpts from THE JERUSALEM BIBLE READER'S EDITION, copyright (c) 1966, 1967, 1968 by Darton, Longman & Todd, Ltd. and Doubleday, a division of Random House, Inc. Reprinted by permission.

Published by James and Kathleen Littleton
P.O. Box 607
Tinley Park, IL 60477
Publishing services provided by Lulu
http://www.lulu.com/

Printed by the fine folks at Lulu (www.lulu.com)

ISBN: 978-1-4303-2398-3

Dedication

Set your hearts on his Kingdom first, and on his righteousness, and all these other things will be given you as well. So do not worry about tomorrow: tomorrow will take care of itself. Each day has enough trouble of its own.
(Matthew 6: 33-34)

The process of writing this book commenced on June 12, 2006, the Eve of the Feast of St. Anthony of Padua.

It was completed and dedicated on Our Lady of the Rosary, First Saturday, October 7, 2006.

This work is consecrated to the Blessed Virgin Mary.

Dedication:

We dedicate this book to our living children: Shannon Rose, Tara Kathleen, Grace Ellen, Colleen Anne, Deirdre Marie, Bridget Jane, Shane Francis, Fiona Mary, Maura Therese, Clare Margaret, Patrick Michael, Mairead Siobhan, Brighde Rosemarie, and Shealagh Maeve.

Dedication

The fruitfulness of this book is placed in the intercessory hands of our team of children in heaven: Maximilian Mary, Theresa Gerard, James Paul, Frances Xavier, and Joseph Faustina Littleton.

We also dedicate this book to you the reader. Though most of us have not met in our present life on earth, we are connected, we are family, and we are one in the Mystical Body of Christ. Let's pray for each other. May we meet joyfully in heaven.

We wish to express our gratitude to our spiritual directors over the years and the many priests and spiritual role models whom God has placed in our path.

We also place the efficacy of this book in the hands of our special heavenly friends:
- St. Joseph
- St. Paul
- St. Pio
- St. Anthony of Padua
- St. Francis of Assisi
- St. Faustina
- St. Therese of the Child Jesus
- St. Maximilian Kolbe
- St. Philomena

Better by the Dozen, Plus Two

- St. Jerome
- St. Thomas More
- St. John Vianney
- St. John Bosco
- St. Rafael Guizar y Valencia
- St. Ignatius of Loyola
- Blessed Junípero Serra
- Blessed José Luis Sánchez del Rio
- Venerable, Walter Ciszek
- Venerable, Solanus Casey
- Venerable, Emil Kapaun
- Servant of God, John Paul the Great
- Servant of God, Archbishop Fulton J. Sheen
- Servant of God, Maura Degollado Guizar
- Servant of God, Mary Theresa Dudzik
- Servant of God, Vincent Capodanno
- Archbishop Luis Martinez
- Fr. Mac (Msgr. Ignatius McDermott)
- St. Michael, the Archangel
- St. Gabriel, the Archangel
- St. Raphael, the Archangel
- All the Blessed Angels, Saints, and Souls in Purgatory.

Pray for us.

Acknowledgements

We would like to thank our spiritual directors, past and present, namely Fr. André LaSana, L.C. and Fr. James Larson, L.C., as well as our pastor, Fr. Tom Corbino for their invaluable support and encouragement over the years. We love you Fr. André, Fr. James and Fr. Tom.

A special thanks to Claudia Volkman for her professional, priceless, and generous advice throughout the publishing process.

A profound thank you to the community of Poor Clares in Lemont, Illinois for their powerful prayers.

Our sincere gratitude to those who bigheartedly took the time from their busy schedules to review our manuscript and write an endorsement: Fr. Joseph D. Fessio, S.J., Kris Cortes, and Mark and Elizabeth Matthews.

Prologue

Courage! It is I! Do not be afraid.
(Matthew: 14: 28)

Over the past twenty years, God has blessed our family with the gift of nineteen children-- fourteen living and five in heaven. We have twelve daughters and two sons living, ranging in age from twenty years to seven months. This book shares the story of how we came to be such a large family and the truths God taught us along the way.

We have had to struggle with many temptations to abandon writing this book as we confront our many inadequacies and the numerous ways we fall short. We are tempted to think that people who know us and our many failings might challenge us as imposters, phonies, and hypocrites, and question how we might dare to write a book offering advice and formation to others. Well, if we waited for the perfect of the world to do the work of promulgating truth and virtue, nothing good would ever be accomplished. We do not wish to attempt to abdicate all personal culpability for our personal failings, but we are convinced it would be a grave and irresponsible sin of omission to leave this little work undone because of our own unworthiness. Moreover, in our own experience we have always found more consolation in, and been more convinced and won over, by the example of those persons who have accomplished great things in life for God and their fellow man, *despite* their human inadequacies and limitations, because they are like us, and we can relate to them. So perhaps the reader will even find some encouragement in our ongoing struggle to live more authentically the very things we preach. We are all human and in need of mercy and a *Redeemer*.

"... It was to shame the wise that God chose what is foolish by human reckoning, and to shame what is strong that he chose what is weak by human reckoning; those whom the world thinks common and contemptible are the ones that God has chosen--those who are nothing at all to show up those who are everything. The human race has nothing to boast about to God, but you God has made members of Christ Jesus and by God's doing he has become our wisdom, and our virtue, and our holiness, and our freedom. As scripture says: *If anyone boasts, let him boast in the Lord.*" (1 Corinthians 1:27-31)

Prologue

It has been very difficult to write about our family, to put ourselves in the spotlight. We would candidly prefer to remain hidden. That would be much easier, much more comfortable, but we have felt a strong calling to share some of the gifts of what we have learned and experienced in our lives with others. "Not that I do boast of preaching the gospel, since it is a duty which has been laid on me; I should be punished if I did not preach it!" (1 Corinthians 9:16-17)

We realized that by mere virtue of the fact we have been blessed with fourteen living children, plus five in heaven, many might be attracted to read what we have to express, if only through initial curiosity. Our infinitely loving God utilizes many mysterious means for our good. We do not consider ourselves masters or prime examples in the subjects we have written on. We try to live the things we preach the best we can, yet, we admit, dreadfully imperfectly. "For it is not ourselves that we are preaching, but Christ Jesus as the Lord." (2 Corinthians 4:5) "We are only the earthenware jars that hold this treasure to make it clear that such an overwhelming power comes from God and not from us." (2 Corinthians 4:7-8)

Our target audience includes all persons of good will. Although we are Catholic, and by the grace of God our faith permeates who we are and everything we do, think and say, we wish to appeal to *secular* as well as religious and Catholic audiences. We do not desire that this book should be classified as *strictly* religious. We would like to reach as many people as possible. Our goal has been to make this an appealing and interesting read for anyone and everyone, to move the reader to serious reflection on the state of his or her life, and to hopefully come away with some helpful *resolutions*, of a spiritual and/or practical nature.

We do encourage the reader to *pray* before reading this book, *pray* while reading it, and to *pray* always. Many aspects of this book can only be truly understood with *supernatural help*. We hope the reader will *pray* to God for this help, for the help of the Holy Spirit. It is also our desire that the reader will take time, as inspired to do so, to open up the Bible and read and reflect further on the scripture that is salted into this work. *Certainly the Holy Spirit has more to say to you than we are able to enumerate in such a limited fashion*. Perhaps the reader will also take the step to

Prologue

read further some of the other writings referenced herein.

We have tried to be open to the work of the Holy Spirit in our writing, not that we are even close to infallible. We are laity. We have no theological degrees, although we have devoured information on our faith over the past many years. We have strived to remain in complete conformity with the Church's teachings. We would never knowingly go against these in any way. We love the Church and *everything* she teaches, no exceptions.

We trust the reader will experience the recurring theme of *hope* in this book. Yes, one encounters many difficulties in life and in the world, many areas we need to work to improve upon in our lives, but *we must rest assured that God is with us. We are totally dependent on him, and he is always faithful. He is in command. We need not be afraid. Not a single detail of our life escapes his loving and beneficent providence.*

If the reader finds himself challenged or in any way discouraged by what he encounters is this work, we implore him to trust in God's *inexhaustible mercy* and help to conform to his will. We are hoping to give the reader what we coin *the two "C's*, to *challenge and console*. We must always *hope*. The past is past. We can learn from it, but we cannot go back. The future is not in our control. God does not want us to bring the anxiety of the future down upon ourselves. All we have is today, the *now*. We must learn to live in the present. God's will can be found there, in the ordinary as well as in the difficulties and disasters of life. We need to advance in faith and hope in order to be at peace.

Through prayer, experiences in helping others in their faith and family formation, and through various comments and encouragement we have received, we have become convinced that an audience would be interested in and benefit in some way from this description of how our family, by the grace of God, strives to live our lives, and in our philosophy of life. We include anecdotes and a philosophy of life from a family of sixteen to give insights into the meaning and purpose of life, with the goal of helping the reader to achieve true happiness and fulfillment. We hope to help readers to reflect on and reexamine a *hierarchy of values* or priorities in the midst of the modern dominant culture which is seriously disordered. We write very simply about what we have come to know primarily though our interior life and practical experience. We have tried to bring out the difficulties and the reality of our lives. The reader will encounter a glimpse into, though not including every superfluous detail, our own Godless, hedonistic, materialistic lives (more so Jim's) before our reversions to our faith. We hope that by sharing these aspects of our past, the reader can better relate to us and to our messages.

We have also included many hopefully humorous and entertaining anecdotes so as to make this an enjoyable read in addition to the more challenging aspects of being a catalyst for some serious reflection relative to areas of the reader's life which may need revision, healing, and redemption.

We don't wish to present ourselves as an anomaly, nor as an ideal example, but we would like to contribute in some way to the authentic comeback of God, then family, as the center of each person's life and of society; giving faith and family (as the fundamental unit of society) their true place in the *hierarchy of values*.

We have done our best to examine the dominant culture unequivocally and identify major aspects of its confusion, lies, and disorder; and then, rather than being content to wring our hands and complain, we attempt to provide some *hopeful*, practical and effective solutions.

Some of the *cultural problems* we have tried to address include:
- What happens when God and his will are not our first and highest concern?
- Prevalence of self-centeredness
- What happens when God is not at the core of marriage?
- Pervasiveness of divorce
- Fear of being open to having more children. Does closing the door to openness to life in marriage really bring the good and happiness longed for?
- Prevalence of seeking to fill our void with stuff. Materialism, how this never satisfies; one always keeps seeking more. This results in a type of modern slavery.
- Prevalence of *haste i*n the dominant culture. People in the dominant culture are rushing constantly, but to what end?
- Great prevalence of fear and lack of real faith. A *fear-driven culture*, a sense of wanting to be in complete control (an impossible goal), rather than a deep abiding faith and trust in God. This induces us

to hate our neighbors, and inspires a readiness to crush anyone that interferes with our false sense of comfort and control, anyone who wants to *intrude into our bubble*. Just listen to talk radio. Divisive. Over and over they shout: "Crucify him!" (John 19:6)

- Prevalent disordered use of the gift of sexuality
- An epidemic of abortion, sterilization, and contraception
- Depression, over medication, infidelity, emptiness
- The family as the center for all the members is non-existent in most families.
- Morally relativistic society; the boiled frog syndrome
- *Today's religion is politics*. People are obsessed with and consumed by politics. But, no particular political ideology alone will solve all societal problems or bring the happiness people innately hunger for.

Some of the solutions and encouragement we propose in this book include:

- Radical problems call for radical solutions. With God's help we must cultivate a willingness to risk, to be *radically d*ifferent than the dominant culture. "You

will shine in the world like bright stars because you are offering it the word of life." (Philippians 2:15)
- We must develop a *supernatural outlook*. We must be people of prayer. Permit God to transform us. *'Martha, Martha,' he said 'you worry and fret about so many things, and yet few are needed, indeed only one. It is Mary who has chosen the better part; it is not to be taken from her.'* (Luke 10:41-42)
- Our children have a great untapped capacity for virtue, sacrifice, and service.
- Cultivate a willingness to *sacrifice*.
- Learn to embrace the difficulties in life. Be thankful for them. What would life be without challenges?
- God will never give us more than we can handle, though we may in moments of weakness mistakenly think that he broke this rule in our case.
- To be happy in any and all circumstances.
- Be open to life; to have faith like Abraham. "Abraham called this place 'Yahweh Provides'." (Genesis 22:14)
- To slow down. When in constant haste we don't have time to reflect on and notice the wonders we have around us to be thankful for, like the innocence of a child's face, God's very image and likeness.

Prologue

- Not to be afraid to make mistakes. He'll provide the graces to do the mission he asks of us. We must merely try our best, without putting undue pressure on ourselves. If we do our best, we can count on God to do the rest.
- Requisite sense of humor.

We hope you will stay with us, that you will stay the course of reading and reflecting on this little work. And may our Blessed Lord be with our spirits. "They pressed him to stay with them." (Luke 24:29)

James & Kathleen Littleton, October 7, 2006
Our Lady of the Rosary, First Saturday

CONTENTS

Dedication i
Acknowledgements v
Prologue vii

Chapter 1 1
  How We Came to Be a Family
Chapter 2 17
  How We Came to Live Our Faith: Jim's Reversion
Chapter 3 29
  Hierarchy of Values
Chapter 4 55
  Marriage
Chapter 5 69
  Motherhood
Chapter 6 85
  Openness to Life
Chapter 7 123
  Miscarriage
Chapter 8 135
  Formation of Children
Chapter 9 193
  Called to Service
Chapter 10 199
  On the Cross
Chapter 11 227
  The Importance of Having a Sense of Humor

Epilogue 251
Abbreviations and Resources 255
About the Authors 257

Chapter 1
How We Came to be a Family

"Happy, all those who fear Yahweh and follow in his paths.

You will eat what your hands have worked for, happiness and prosperity will be yours.

Your wife: a fruitful vine on the inner walls of your house.

Your sons: round your table like shoots round an olive tree.

Such are the blessings that fall on the man who fears Yahweh."

(Psalm 128:1-4)

Jim and I (Kathleen) grew up living a mile away from each other but never knew it for two decades. Then we met. It was not love at first sight, at least for me. Jim tells me it was for him.

I was twenty and a third year university student, planning to attend law school upon graduation. Jim was twenty-one and a high school graduate, at the time working as a supervisor on a loading dock.

Jim recalls, "Although I had seen Kathleen casually around the neighborhood a few times in my late teenage years, the first time I really took note of her was at a party at the university where Kathleen was attending. I saw her across the room. It was truly a moment of profound grace, although I could not label it at that time. Somehow I knew, and had a deep interior certainty that Kathleen would be my wife. I told my friend, Dan, 'See that girl, she's going to be my bride.' Whenever I saw her from that time forward, I would refer to her as my bride, which Kathleen found, needless to say, very strange, but I think somewhat amusing and intriguing. I had very little prayer life (I would pray to win big pots in poker games and such) and almost no understanding of the things of God at that time, although in retrospect, I see God's hand in this experience. I am convinced that *he reached down and touched my soul*. He had a plan for me, for Kathleen, for our children yet to be born, for all those we would come in contact with and influence in our lives, for the many generations of our family yet to come, for all those who will be touched by them, and perhaps for you, the reader, to come into contact with this book. God has plans, very significant plans, for each of us in our lives. Everyone's life and mission is essential, irreplaceable."

We had both been raised on the south side of Chicagoland, both from Irish Catholic middle class families, which made us what is termed there proudly, "Southside Irish." In this neighborhood and parish-centered sense of family, everyone was Irish, even if you really weren't.

Jim is the oldest of five children, and I am the fourth of six. Both our parents were faithful, practicing Catholics, attending Sunday Mass regularly and mine were very involved in parish life. We both attended Catholic parochial elementary schools and continued on to our local single-sex Catholic liberal arts high schools. Here is where the parallels end.

Jim chose to leave the Catholic high school in the middle of his third year, having difficulty seeing any sense in the strictness of the rules, already manifesting his rebellious and choleric temperament. He completed his final courses at the local public high school while working menial jobs, including assistant manager of a karate school.

He moved out on his own at age eighteen. Jim worked as a janitor, cleaning offices and dumping garbage in a downtown Chicago office building for about a year. He then went to work part-time on the loading docks for United Parcel Service, eventually being promoted to part-time supervisor. His employment at UPS lasted for five years. During this time, Jim admits his main focus was earning enough money to pay the rent, have a car, buy groceries, and have sufficient cash for partying. "I was a hedonist. I would have been a materialist as well if I had enough money." Jim would make it to Sunday Mass during these years, sporadically, as long as he was not too hungover, sleeping past the last Mass, which was quite often.

I, on the other hand, finished high school with high grades, a high class rank, and went on to pursue a degree at a large state university. And so we met there, three years later, through a mutual friend that Jim was visiting one weekend. We didn't actually really meet each other. He saw me, but I didn't even know he was there. As I said, it was not love at first sight on my part. I had no interest in someone who wasn't pursuing higher education, the intellectual snob that I was, and wrote him off even without really ever even talking to him.

How We Came to be a Family

Time passed, I graduated, and was back living at home preparing to enter law school in the fall. We met again at the wake of a mutual friend. My heart softened to him due to the circumstances, and somehow I found myself very much wanting to get to know him better. We started dating and I soon realized he was the one. On Christmas Eve, a year and a half later, we became engaged to be married. My parents were very concerned about the disparity of our educations (and Jim did not win any points when he tongue–in-cheek asked my father what the word *disparity* meant), but nothing can keep me from doing God's will when I know what it is he wants me to do. Jim was convinced all along. Together, we had no doubts and never have.

I recall around this time standing in a bar, talking to Jim about how many children we would like to have someday. We both agreed we should have a large family, and came up with the seemingly very large number of five! Neither of us ever dreamed we would meet that goal in the next seven years, let alone far surpass that number. We have been truly blessed. Our children are a gift from God, and with that gift comes a great responsibility. To those to whom God has given much, much will be asked of.

We were married, I completed law school, passed the bar exam, and began working in a Chicago loop law firm. Jim obtained a position in the insurance industry. We were very happy. We attended Mass on Sundays, when it was convenient, but that was the extent of our faith life. Truly, that was it. Of course we believed in God, but other than a vague sense of owing him something on Sundays, we went about living our lives in a manner that seemed fine to us at the time. That included staying out late drinking with friends most every weekend, and even more serious in hindsight and gravely wrong, using the birth control pill to prevent pregnancy. I wanted to pursue my law career and had law school loans to pay off. Jim admits that he would have continued to postpone the start of a family indefinitely due to the lack of financial resources. We both felt we were doing the logical thing, the right thing, what was expected of us, and the decision to start on that large family was selfishly put off without much thought.

Then, the grace of God intervened. To this day, I don't even know how it happened. I attribute it solely to the Holy Spirit. Little by little, I began to feel that somehow it was wrong to be putting off having a baby.

And it seemed wrong somehow to me to be taking birth control pills. Jim and I were ignorant and indifferent that this was against the Church's teaching. We had never been told that, not by our parents, not during Pre-Cana which is a marriage preparation weekend course, not by a priest, not by anyone.

I wanted a family, and I know Jim did too. Actually, that was one of the reasons I fell in love with him because I had seen him around children and how good he was with them, and I imagined him being like that with our own children someday. My law job was challenging and not fulfilling me as I thought it would. I wanted more. Actually, I didn't want more, I wanted something else. I wanted to have a baby, and I knew Jim did too.

So one day, I just stopped taking the pills. I don't know if I even told Jim. Jim recalls that I didn't, although he was exceedingly grateful that I took this action. And I didn't worry about it. As a matter of fact, I even forgot that I had stopped taking them. Time passed, exactly four and a half months to be exact. I remember, because when the doctor diagnosed what I thought was a thyroid problem because I was gaining weight, he told me I was twenty-weeks pregnant. That was my shortest and easiest pregnancy, because it was half over by the time I knew I was even expecting!

When Jim heard the news that I was expecting, he was extremely happy. We were both thrilled, and wondered why we had closed ourselves off to this essential aspect of our marriage for so long. We named her Shannon Rose. *That was twenty years and nineteen children ago.*

Jim felt that since we had one child, why not have another. He was not especially pro-life or out to be fertile and multiply, but reasoned that since life had changed so drastically with one child so that we could not come and go as we pleased, why not have another. This kind of thinking kept us going until our fifth child was born. Our awesome God works in mysterious and wonderful ways.

Tara Kathleen was born fifteen months after Shannon, then Grace Ellen, fourteen months after Tara. Colleen Anne was born one year and three weeks after Grace, and so I had two babies to carry as neither could walk yet! Shannon was not yet four years old when our fourth daughter was born.

The saddest and most unexpected day came when I experienced my first miscarriage. I still can feel the emotional pain and loss of the baby we later named Maximilian Mary. There is a space there, a gap not just in years before the next child, but in my heart. I didn't think I would ever be able to have another baby, and I was devastated.

And so it was with great joy that I saw Deirdre's heartbeat on the screen of the ultrasound machine at thirteen weeks gestation! Baby girl number five was born, almost two years after Colleen. At this time, Jim began his reversion to the Catholic faith which is referenced in the next chapter.

The next baby came just over a year later, our sixth daughter in a row, Bridget Jane. Now our family totaled six children under age six, all girls. I had given up the idea of ever having a son, believing that somehow Jim and I weren't capable of conceiving a male child. And so, I resorted to some supernatural help. I decided to pray a nine-day novena to the Blessed Mother. I don't recall ever having prayed a novena before, and didn't really know how to do it, so I made it a very spontaneous prayer that went something like, "Dear Mary, please tell God that I would love to have another baby, and if it is God's will, please let it be a boy. If it is, I promise to give this baby back to him. He will be his to do with as he will." Surprisingly enough, Shane was conceived the next month. Our first son! For years later, I could still marvel at the fact of his existence. My prayer had been answered, and I would remember my promise. Actually, Shane himself wouldn't let me forget it.

I found out about my next pregnancy in a rather unexpected manner. Being very sick with a chest cold, I went to the doctor to see if I could get some antibiotics. He decided I needed a chest x-ray, but first asked me if there was any possibility of me being pregnant. I responded, "With me, there is always that possibility." And so, I had a pregnancy test done. When the doctor told me I was indeed pregnant, I told him, "I'd rather be sick!" And I wasn't kidding. I admit I was not happy to be pregnant again. I thought our family was sufficiently complete in my opinion. Jim always was ready for another baby, and I knew he'd be thrilled. Gradually, as the baby grew within me, I too began to appreciate this gift I'd been given again, and looked forward to welcoming another child. By the time Fiona Mary was born, I was completely ready for her, and wondered how I could ever have had such feelings of ingratitude.

How We Came to be a Family

God was soon going to reveal to me a deeper lesson on the value of life. It came in the form of my second miscarriage. Shortly after Fiona's birth I found myself pregnant again, and very happy about it. Within a few weeks, however, I miscarried this baby, Theresa Gerard, leaving me even more determined and desirous to again experience the gift of life, a gift I would never again take for granted, or fail to appreciate. God had taught me my lesson well. And he rewarded me too in the following way for my surrender to his will.

I again conceived, but at six weeks started spotting, the first signs, at least for me, of another miscarriage. Jim went with me to the hospital for an early ultrasound at six weeks gestation to find out what was happening. He knew I would be very upset if I was losing this baby. The ultrasound technician wouldn't tell me anything, but called in a doctor. By now, I was very fearful. Not only am I having a miscarriage, but there must be something else very seriously wrong, I believed. The doctor came and went, and still they wouldn't tell us what was going on. Finally, they told us the news ... no, I wasn't having a miscarriage, I was having twins! Two baby heartbeats appeared on the screen, and I was overjoyed! I always wanted to have twins, two for the price of one! I never dreamed though, they would come as number nine and ten! Jim was happy, but very worried for my health. I didn't give it a thought. I was basking in this delightful, miraculous, totally thrilling reality.

Reality took a while to sink in. Even when my doctor told me that preterm labor with twins was very common and very serious, I didn't take him seriously. After all, I had given birth to eight children by now, and all of them had come on or very near their due dates, never early. That wouldn't happen to me.

And so, when I went into labor with the twins at twenty-eight weeks, I thought it was just labor as usual. Time to have the babies! Again, the reality of what was happening took a while to sink in. It wasn't until I was at the hospital hooked up to the monitors, that the full impact of what was happening hit me. I still couldn't understand why I couldn't just have the babies, and so the doctors had to convince me by giving me a very vivid picture. Yes, I was in labor, but if I delivered the babies then, the babies may not survive.

And so the battle began, the battle to keep the babies. It was long and arduous, full of medication, bed rest, medical tests, human error, prayer, and miracles.

How We Came to be a Family

At thirty-four weeks, the twins were born, Maura and Clare. Clare thrived and came home. Maura didn't. Put on a ventilator as she couldn't breathe on her own, she contracted bacterial meningitis as well as a yeast infection thru her system a few days after her birth. Thus ensued days and long nights of fear, the unknown, infections, spinal taps, blood transfusions, middle-of-the-night long drives to the hospital leaving her days old twin sister at home with daddy, prayer and more prayer, unexpected hope and the dashing of hope, a dark prognosis that if she survived she had little chance of living a normal life, and finally, six weeks later, the reunion of the twins on the day Maura, beating all the odds through the grace of God, healthy at last, came home! What joy and thanksgiving! God has been so good to us!

For the month I was in the hospital on bed rest before delivering the twins, with eight children at home ages twelve and under, out of necessity Jim devised the plan of delegation that we still use today. Realizing that I wasn't going to be around to do everything I did before, for an unknown length of time, Jim divided up all my chores amongst the children who were of an age to do them. *Children are much more capable than we generally give them credit for.* The *Littleton Family Manual* was created. The manual includes work responsibilities and time schedules for the children for mornings, after school and evenings, Saturday mornings, kitchen assignments, homework tracking tables, a flow chart for charges and charge-masters (as referred to in the *Formation of Children* chapter) and family house rules. The system has been tweaked and modified to such perfection like clockwork over the years, so that even today, I can be gone for short or long periods of time, and the household runs smoothly, and I will be the first to admit, often even more efficiently than if I was there.

Soon after the twins were born came another pregnancy, and another sorrow when at my sixteen-week check up the doctor was unable to find a heartbeat. The baby had died in my womb and the explanation came upon seeing the perfect little body with the umbilical cord twisted repeatedly around his neck. Yes, our second son. We named him James Paul.

But God is good, and as has been said, he never closes a door without opening a window; another pregnancy, and this time, another miracle. God gave us another son, a beautiful healthy, baby boy, Patrick Michael, our eleventh living child.

Two years passed. Thinking my fertility had waned, I recall saying that I believed Patrick would be our last child. I was forty years old. God had other plans, though, and I conceived Mairead Siobhan, another perfect baby. Then followed two more early miscarriages, Frances Xavier and Joseph Faustina, then two more healthy babies, Brighde Rosemarie and almost exactly one year later, when I was forty-six years old, Shealagh Maeve, our fourteenth living child and our nineteenth all together, counting our five babies in heaven.

I marvel as I look at all my children, and hold these two new beautiful babies, why have we been so especially blessed with so many children? And all I can think in response is what an incredible gift and what an awesome responsibility!

What all is God asking of us? Will we be able to fulfill his plans for us? And I know in my heart that we will, if we stay close to him! That is my prayer every day, "Give me the grace of perseverance and fidelity to the mission you have entrusted to me, that I don't get in your way, and that you do with me what you will." For that is what *love is: total self-giving*, wanting only what God wants, and doing it. That is the kind of love *I aspire to*, a Christ-like love. It is the kind of love all persons are called to aspire to, in imitation of Christ. This is a profound *gift* that we must ask for, *count on*, and cooperate with.

Chapter 2
How We Came to Live Our Faith: Jim's Reversion

I am the living bread which has come down from heaven. Anyone who eats this bread will live forever; and the bread that I shall give is my flesh, for the life of the world.
(John 6:51)

Our blessed Lord always has our unique mission in mind and will orchestrate events to occur in accordance with his providence to help us to discover and to *choose* to live his plan (James). He invites us to respond in freedom and in love. In my case, despite my rebellion, sinfulness, and indifference through much of my life, he laid the groundwork for my reversion to the Catholic faith, which was to begin at age thirty-three.

I had grown up Catholic in a Catholic family, but my Catholicism and faith were for the most part superficial. I attended Catholic grammar school as well as Catholic high school through the middle of junior year. As a child, through grammar school, I attended Mass every Sunday with a sense of obligation, but that was about it. I had no other real prayer life. Although my parents, wonderful sacrificial people, with the best of intentions, sent my siblings and me to Catholic grammar school and some to Catholic high school, there was little or no family prayer outside of Sunday Mass. My parents did, however set a matchless example of marital love and respect for each other, and sacrificial love and service for their children. Their exemplary lives and actions speak volumes, and they will always be a benchmark that I fall far short of. In line with the dominant culture of the time, I think my parents sincerely believed they were fulfilling their duty to provide a religious formation by seeing that we received a Catholic education, and that that would take care of our faith essentials. I think that one of the big widespread errors of the time was to see the Catholic faith as, for the most part, fulfilling an obligation to God as opposed to developing a more personal relationship based on love.

One can never underestimate human ingenuity in terms of finding ways to get around the legalism of the law. But when one loves, one is not a minimalist. One who loves is not concerned merely with fulfilling an obligation, but rather wants to do everything possible to make the beloved happy. If one loves his wife, he does not tell her "See, I love you, as I have not murdered you, stolen from you, beaten you, or lied to you." One goes out of his way to find ways to make his wife happy. He would not dream of seriously offending her, but does not stop there. He will support her, spend time with her, buy her flowers and candy, and go so far as to lay down his life for her. Our relationship with God must be based on *love*. The Church is not an institution; it is not *something*, it is *someone*, a *person*, namely Jesus Christ.

Retrospectively, I do recall some instances in my childhood that were perhaps a precursor to the gift of making my faith my own, which I was to receive much later in adulthood. I vaguely recall having an innate realization of, and attraction to, the real presence of Christ in the Eucharist, and a love for the Mass. I seem to recall in late grammar school that I once went to daily Mass about forty days in a row. But, once I was in eighth grade and beyond, I was on the road to being a complete, self-centered hedonist. I would fool myself that I was doing alright with God, who I fundamentally believed in, as I had not murdered anyone. My Sunday

Mass attendance was sporadic, and the Sacrament of Reconciliation or Confession was totally off the radar screen.

As I progressed through my party years and then into marriage, I was definitely a minimalist when it came to God. I was completely assimilated into the dominant culture. From the time Kathleen and I were married and during the early years as we began raising a family, most people who knew me would probably say that I was a decent man doing his duty of providing for his family. But the dominant culture's definition of a decent man is not necessarily God's definition, and it was certainly not God's definition when it came to me. The scary thing is that I thought I was doing fine. Knowing what I know now, I realize that I was breaking every commandment on a regular basis. I was blind and deaf in terms of knowing myself, and the state I was in.

But, our merciful Father in heaven does not give up on anyone. So, when I had been married already for about eight years, there was a report that the Blessed Virgin Mary was appearing at a local cemetery in the Chicago area. This fascinated me as I had retained a belief in the supernatural from my youth, as well as a fondness towards Our Lady. I packed Kathleen and our five children at the time in the car and went to see what it was all about, hoping beyond hope that I would be privileged to see the Blessed Virgin Mary or some sort of miracle. The real motivation for doing this was a self-centered curiosity, hoping for a dazzling sign, but God will use even means like this to draw us to him.

We went to the cemetery a couple times as I recall. I was grasping at signs, thinking that perhaps an outline in the bark of a tree was an image of the Blessed Virgin Mary. While I did not witness any concrete signs or miracles, something much more subtle and profound occurred. I recall experiencing an internal awareness and consolation of the presence of God, and I believe, the Blessed Mother. It was very real, but I did not understand it. I was also profoundly impressed with the faith and prayerfulness of many of the people present. I was amazed at their faith and conviction. I was very attracted to this.

As I recall, a woman handed me a card. On this card were listed the fifteen promises of the Blessed Virgin Mary to those who pray the rosary. I found these promises fascinating. So I dutifully took this card, placed it on my dresser, and left it there for many months, perhaps even for a year, before picking up a rosary to pray. From time to time I would pass by this holy card and think that I really should pray the rosary, but I did not act.

Eventually I decided to do so. I did not even know how to pray the rosary, nor did I remember the prayers. I obtained a pamphlet on how to pray the rosary, and literally had to read the prayers because I could not remember them. I started by praying one decade a day in the car, which consists of one *Our Father*, ten *Hail Mary's* and a *Glory Be*. I would turn the radio off on the way to work long enough to pray these prayers, which probably took about one or two minutes. This duration was a major challenge for me taking me to the limit of my perseverance in prayer. I found it hard to believe that people could pray this much in a single day.

What happened from there can only be explained supernaturally. I can now attest to the fact that once the Blessed Mother takes hold of a soul, she will always bring him to Christ in the most rapid way possible. From the humble beginnings, by the grace of God, of praying one decade of the rosary, I quickly progressed to praying five decades of the rosary per day, and *then it happened*. Something, or rather *Someone*, moved me to get up one morning and go to a Mass (daily Mass) during the week. I went to the morning Mass at our local parish. Again, this is something that can only be explained supernaturally. I was overcome, conquered by the presence of God. This reality could not be denied. I could not hold back the tears. Our Blessed Lord and his mother, Mary, had poured out a tremendous grace upon me. This was all their doing. It was all God's grace.

From this moment, I began to be a regular daily Mass attendee. As best I can recall, I started out attending Mass several days a week but not every day. The graces I received through the rosary and the Eucharist led me to begin to learn more about my faith. When I came to realize how special the Eucharist is, which I can now theologically explain as being the "source and summit of the Christian life," (CCC 1324) I knew that I needed to attend Mass every day. Initially, in my mind "every day" excluded Saturday, as I reasoned the Lord would surely understand that I needed to sleep in on Saturdays. Eventually I understood that I was being called to attend Mass every day, no exceptions.

A parishioner lent me a cassette tape on the Holy Hour, by Servant of God, Archbishop Fulton J. Sheen.

As I recall, this is what led me to begin regular Eucharistic adoration, which is spending time in the presence of Jesus truly present, Body, Blood, Soul, and Divinity, in the Eucharist.

The Lord also blessed me with the realization that if daily Mass was essential for me, blessing me with infinite graces, then how could I leave my children at home? So I started bringing all my children to Mass on a daily basis with the exception of those in diapers who were left at home with Kathleen who had not *yet* surrendered to the graces of daily Mass attendance.

During this time we began incorporating daily prayer, including the rosary, into our family life. This was a tremendous blessing. By the grace of God we naturally wanted to share what we had received, and would evangelize by inviting other families to join us for prayer. Many ignored our invitations, but some accepted, and by God's grace we were given the *privilege* to, in some way, be God's instruments in helping these families grow in their faith.

Eventually Kathleen began to attend Mass daily, and we brought even the babies. Kathleen had attended one weekday Mass and received the grace to never turn back. And so, for about the last seven years, we have attended Mass every day with every single member of our family. Even now with some of our older children dispersed at schools around the country, they each continue their daily Mass attendance. So, although we are not usually all at the same Mass, we are all at Mass every day, and therefore united in this sublime way.

Our family's daily Mass attendance is a testament to the grace that God has given us to primarily be able to recognize, and secondly to be able to live a proper *hierarchy of values*. This is a beautiful grace, a gift that we want to share with the reader. We know we must give God first place in our lives. We also unequivocally believe as Catholics that the Mass is the re-presentation of the passion, death and resurrection of our Lord Jesus Christ and that we are mystically present at and in these events at every Mass. We know that the Eucharist is truly the Body, Blood, Soul and Divinity of Jesus Christ, God and Man. There is no greater means available on earth to be with, receive, and be incorporated into Jesus Christ than the Eucharist. Therefore, how could we not give this Sacrament first place in our lives, *every day*? What obstacle or difficulty would be too great to do everything in our power to overcome so as to prevent us from missing even one Mass?

We have been given an enormous gift, the grace of living Eucharistic lives, and I rejoice in sharing with the reader the unlikely and miserable *hunk of clay* the Lord poured his blessings upon in me. *It is all God's work. But I see this as a gift that must be shared.*

Early on in my reversion I was also brought, by the grace of God, to frequenting the Sacrament of Reconciliation, also called Confession. For many years now our entire family has gone to confession on a weekly basis. This has been a tremendous grace. There is no remission of sin without the shedding of blood. To paraphrase as I recall hearing on an unknown recording from Servant of God, Archbishop Fulton J. Sheen (I often paraphrase him), *when the priest, in the person of Christ raises his hand and pronounces the words of absolution, Christ's blood is mystically dripping from his hand*. The penitent's sins are washed away and forgotten, as if they never existed. He is restored to God's grace and strengthened in future battles to avoid sin and live virtue.

Through my reversion, it took many years to gradually come to know myself and recognize the sin in various areas of my life. With God's help I have gradually whittled away at these areas. My conversion is ongoing, as with the Divine assistance, I continue to see myself more and more in the light of God, and in the truth that God sees me; and I continue to strive to *crowd* out my various sins and faults with God's grace, and to live a life of virtue. It is all God's work with which I feebly, but essentially cooperate with, thanks be to our merciful God.

As Kathleen, our children and I continued to grow in grace, we became more and more involved in practical means of sharing the gift of faith we have received. It is all a privilege. We have been given so much, and have a great sense of duty and mission to share what we have received. Therefore we are writing this book for the glory of God and the greater good of all persons of good will. Anything good in it is God's work. Anything lacking is from us.

Chapter 3
Hierarchy of Values

"Only Jesus."
(Mark 9:9)

Since our reversion to the faith, God has moved us to accept what we believe are his *hierarchy of values*. Simply, they are the following, with the first having the highest value (James):

- God
- Spouse
- Children
- Work
- Service Work or Apostolate

We firmly believe that every decision and every aspect of our lives should be based on this *hierarchy of values*. Few would argue that in the United States life has taken on a frantic pace. People in the culture are running in haste, but to where? It seems they have not stopped to evaluate and reflect upon a *hierarchy of values*, and why their time is being consumed by an overabundance of activity.

This seems to us to be a type of modern slavery. People are slaves to many things such as taxiing their children to numerous activities, materialism, hedonism, worship of the golf ball, television, computers, the internet; being slaves to their plan to retire as early as possible, thinking themselves to be secure and comfortable while waiting to expire. But then what?

There is a pervasiveness of fear in general. *Fear paralyzes*. People in today's dominant culture want to be in control of everything including their health, finances, or whatever provides them with a sense of comfort; so they turn in on themselves becoming self-centered and paralyzed. *This is a form of madness because the truth is that we are really not in control. God is in control.* Certainly we should be prudent and do that which is in our power to take care of ourselves, our families, and others, but with a reliance on Almighty God who is beyond doubt in control.

We have each been given talents from our Heavenly Father, and we must give him permission to crowd out our fears with his Holy Spirit, the sweet guest of our souls. This is vitally important as it determines whether we will fulfill the mission God has given to each of us. Note the *Parable of the Talents*. Why did the last servant to be judged receive a severe rebuke from his master? He had gone off and hid the master's talent in the ground. Why? He told the master why: "I was afraid." (Matthew 25:25) When we read this parable it may strike us that this servant's fear was irrational. What did he have to be afraid of? The answer to this question is the same for the servant in the parable as it is for us: *nothing*. We have nothing to fear in following Christ other than suffering a little *medicinal humiliation* and the reality check of coming out of our *ridiculous self-centeredness* to a Christ-centeredness and other-centeredness that holds potential and rewards beyond one's imagination.

In our dominant culture today the family is no longer the center for all of the members. A cohesive family life is nonexistent in many if not most families any more. Many would be hard pressed to offer an explanation as to why they devote so much time and energy to, for example, their children's extracurricular activities. There does not seem to be time to do what is important, or to even reflect on what is important. Often times individuals would admit that, for example, they would like to make it to church, and that they realize that they should, but claim there is no time.

We have a word of advice for anyone who claims to not have time for something they know is important. *Pretend that you died.* The truth is that we are all going to die, and when that time comes, as important as we think we and our things are, the world will go on. It will continue to revolve on its axis. People in our familial, professional, and social circles will have to make some adjustments, but they will all go on. Consider making time for prayer or attendance at church, for example. Pretend that you died, do what you know is important, give God first place, and you will not only come back *risen from the dead*, but you will be *new and improved*.

By the grace of God, we have made a priority in our family *never* to miss *daily* Mass, *never* to miss weekly confession, and *never* to miss family evening prayer. We make frequent Eucharistic visits, spending time in silence before our Blessed Lord in prayer and reflection. These are opportunities for us to assimilate Christ. We would not trade them for the world, and we don't, *ever*. This might sound overwhelming; however, we know that *we are receiving infinitely more than we are giving.*

Kathleen and I would literally rather have our children miss school than miss Mass on any given day, and in fact when a rare conflict has arisen, we have

Hierarchy of Values

brought our children to Mass, and then to school late. This was an easy decision to make considering the fact that by the grace of God, we have a well-defined *hierarchy of values*, and we truly do believe that this hierarchy is universally and objectively true. *It is not something we are constantly reevaluating. It is set in rock, and that rock is Christ.*

Any wisdom and knowledge we have received is an unmerited gift from God. The graces we have received from daily Mass, frequent confession, and a consistent prayer life are beyond measure. Although living this may seem an impossible task to many, our encouragement is to simply try it. You will learn from your own experience the tremendous graces and changes that come into your life and you will be hooked as we are. Scales will fall from your eyes and you will be able to see. *Believe me, if someone had suggested to me before my reversion that we would be living the sacramental and prayer life that we are today, I would have most certainly thought that person was crazy.* If God can work with me, as far away as I was from living according to his will, and as unlikely a candidate as I was, he can work with you.

And we should not be afraid to bring our children to church. So what if they make a little noise. Jesus said, "Let the little children alone, and do not stop them coming to me." (Matthew 19:14) Several years back I wrote the following reflection on the subject of bringing children to daily Mass, which I have shared with a few folks as a means of encouragement:

***

Daily Mass

If we truly, interiorly believe in the Eucharist, and the infinite graces God bestows on us through this sublime Sacrament, then why would we ever miss daily Mass? What are our priorities? And if we attend daily Mass why would we ever not bring our children with? And if we argue that we should at least wait to bring the children along until they are of age to receive Holy Communion, does not a child, in the natural order, receive the effects of the sun from a distance? And if we argue that very young children cannot comprehend the Eucharist, do we adults really fully comprehend this sublime mystery? And if we did, would we not die from such complete knowledge of God's infinite love? And does one have to have an advanced knowledge of science, or any knowledge at all, to receive, in the natural order, the effects of the sun? And if our children misbehave, are they any different than any other child ever born, excepting Christ and his own Mother? And could Christ have possibly made our children imperfect while at the same time excluding them from the transforming graces of the Mass? And did Christ not say, "Let the children come unto me?" And do we realize that the infinite graces of one Mass have more value than all the works ever done by mankind? And do we realize that our works have no transcendent value unless grafted on to the vine of Christ? And if we realize that Christ and his Blessed Mother are calling us to daily Mass attendance as a complete family, why don't we just start? And then why don't we just persevere? And when we realize how truly weak and powerless we are, why don't we beg Christ for the graces we need to do this? Oh, and ask his Blessed Mother to make a special delivery of this prayer!

***

Continuing with the hierarchy of values, the rationale behind putting your spouse before your children is detailed in the "Marriage" chapter. It should go without saying that our children come before our work. As a matter of fact they are one of the primary reasons why we work. But, in practice one can often tend to put the means before the end, work before one's children.

Note that, as essential as it is, work always comes after God, spouse, and children. Work is essential, but it must be balanced so as not to disorder these priorities and values. "'Martha, Martha,' he said 'you worry and fret about so many things, and yet few are needed, indeed only one. It is Mary who has chosen the better part; it is not to be taken away from her.'" (Matthew 10:38-42)

Volunteer or faith based service work is important. I believe that every able-bodied person should be engaged in this at some level according to their possibilities. (Those that are not able-bodied can pray and offer their crosses as a service par excellence.) Service work should never, however, happen in such an imbalanced or extreme way that it negatively impacts a higher priority or value in a significant way. There will always be some tensions between the various priorities as the dynamics of our lives are always changing, however we need to be *constantly reevaluating and making adjustments to live according to our hierarchy of values* for our good, the good of our families, and the good of those God permits us to encounter in our lives.

HIERARCHY OF VALUES

One of my favorite saints is Saint Faustina. She wrote a prayer at the beginning of her famous diary, "Oh my God, when I look into the future, I am frightened, but why plunge into the future? Only the present moment is precious to me as the future may never enter my soul at all. It is no longer in my power to change, correct, or add to the past; for neither sages nor prophets could do that. And so, what the past has embraced I must entrust to God. O present moment, you belong to me, whole and entire. I desire to use you as best I can. And although I am weak and small, you grant me the grace of your omnipotence. So, trusting in your mercy, I walk through life like a little child, offering You each day this heart burning with love for your greater glory." (*Diary, Divine Mercy in My Soul*, by Saint Sister M. Faustina Kowalska, # 2)

Prayer needs to be an integral, relevant part of our daily lives. Our lives must be *prayer driven*. Jesus says that we must be like *little children* to enter the Kingdom of Heaven. (Cf: Luke 18:17) *How and why do we lose our childlike simplicity, and goodness?* Why do we as adults tend to get burned out, old in spirit, fearful, and despondent? On a pragmatic level, of course, this is due to our finite condition wherein our physical and mental capacities diminish over time. This is connected to original sin. "As a result of original sin, human nature is weakened in its powers; subject to ignorance, suffering, and the domination of death..." (CCC 418) It is also related to our participation in the redemptive cross of Jesus. "It makes me happy to suffer for you, as I am suffering now, and in my own body to do what I can to make up all that has still to be undergone by Christ for the sake of his body, the Church." (Colossians 1:24) Our getting physically old is as unavoidable as is our personal death.

On the other hand, why would Christ tell us that we must be like little children, if that was not possible? We can see that it is undeniably possible when we look at people like Blessed Mother Theresa of Calcutta and so many others throughout the Church's history and among those currently living. Most of us have encountered people like this. They have retained and even grown in a childlike goodness, simplicity, peace, and trust. These are happy people who find joy in serving others. What is their secret? I maintain that their secret is that they are people of prayer.

So many people in the dominant culture today are running through life, consumed with activity. They become burnt out, despondent, fearful, and angry. Despite all their activity, their meaningful, transcendent accomplishments tend to be little compared to the childlike, like Blessed Mother Theresa of Calcutta who was energized by her prayer life. Do you know that despite the monumental humanitarian work that she accomplished, she always put God first? She had an intense, constant and consistent prayer life, as do all of the sisters in her congregation. She, as the sisters in her congregation still do, attended Mass every day and spent at least an hour praying before Jesus in the Blessed Sacrament, not to mention their continuous prayer life throughout the day.

It is only through prayer that we can be childlike. Through prayer we develop a complete confidence in God, our Heavenly Father, who is in command and interested in every detail of our lives. We lose our disordered fear. What child when held in his father's arms is fearful? As that child gazes into his father's loving eyes, would the child ever flail and think, "Will he drop me?"

We are body, soul, and spirit. *We were not designed for constant activity without true rest.* Christ tells us, "You must come away to some lonely place all by yourselves and rest for a while; for there were so many coming and going that the apostles had no time even to eat." (Mark 6:31-32) Sound familiar? *This is just as important, in fact more important, than so many of the consuming activities that we think we cannot do without.* People are literally killing themselves, body, soul, and spirit through unremitting activity without prayer. We need to give back time every day for prayer.

Every night we go to sleep is a small death, but with prayer every morning, every new day, *every moment is a new birth*. All is new. There is a horizon of hope before us. We need to give the best of our time to Almighty God so that he can heal us, strengthen us, invigorate us, renew us, fill us so that *I can once again be the real me* that is still there, hidden, suppressed, residing deep inside my heart.

Through prayer God reveals to us what is really essential and important in life. He reveals to us our mission, and gives us the grace to fulfill it. He gives us the power and strength to live according to a true hierarchy of values, to find a true balance in our lives. We can never get to this point with our activity and our efforts alone. *We need God. We need prayer* because this is where we encounter him, our All.

In terms of placing God first, there are other areas in our family's lives that he has helped bring into conformity to his will.

God has first place on Sundays. Sunday is a day of prayer, rest, and family unity. This is in keeping with the commandment of keeping the Sabbath holy. We have to keep in mind that the commandments are not there to oppress us, but rather to help us to be happy and to grow closer to God. This commandment seems to have been pushed aside as irrelevant today. Sundays are treated as another packed day of catching up on chores, to-do lists, work, and shopping. Although there is nothing wrong with having the fun of engaging in some sports activities on Sunday, we are convinced that, for example, it is disordered to have competitive games scheduled on Sunday morning. This makes it much more challenging for people to get to religious services, divides families, and *keeps them harried*. The opportunity is lost for the physical, mental, psychological, and spiritual rest and rejuvenation that *God programmed us to need*.

People return to their normal Monday schedule in an exhausted state. They wonder what happened to their weekend. When you ask them what they did on the weekend their response is often an exasperated, "It was busy!" Parents who sincerely love their children and believe they are giving them the best by keeping them involved in a plethora of activities become totally spent.

When extracurricular activities are dividing the family, this is disordered and will not lead to peace and happiness, even though this was the original well-intentioned goal. We have to pull back and reflect upon what we are expending ourselves on. If so much energy and activity is not achieving the desired results, it is time to forge a new plan, make radical choices, and be willing to act on them. Otherwise, continuing to do the same thing while getting the same results is indeed a form of insanity. *Everything worthwhile in life costs something. We must be willing to pay the bargain price on trading something of an inferior value for something worth much more.*

A further way of keeping with our *hierarchy of values* is that we have spiritual guidance appointments with our children. We try to do this once a month. Kathleen or I will take each child aside individually and ask how their spiritual life is going, we *listen*, and we try to offer helpful insights and guidance. We try to end with a resolution. These one-on-one meetings with a parent also offer the opportunity for general discussions on what is happening in that child's life, or even gripes he or she may have. Of course, the main protagonist in these spiritual guidance meetings is the Holy Spirit. The experience is always very fruitful, and often sublime.

All parents are innately given the grace of state to spiritually form and assist their children. Certainly we should educate and form ourselves to the best of our ability in order to fulfill this responsibility; however, regardless of where we are in this process, we have been given the graces to help and to form our children. We do not need to wait until we are "experts" on our faith or on the interior life.

People have asked us at what age one should begin to give spiritual guidance to one's children. We truly believe that this starts when the child is in the womb. At that point we can help the child through our love and prayers which are mystically transferred to the child. We are convinced that children often respond to the voice and touch of their parents while in the womb.

When the child is an infant, one can do things like whispering the name of Jesus in his or her ear, holding up a religious icon or crucifix to the baby to see and to perhaps to kiss. Our infants and other children respond very blissfully when we walk into their rooms at night and bless them with holy water. Young children are visual and tactile learners. For example, Kathleen, I, or one of the children will carry our infants around the church showing them various devotional things like the Stations of the Cross and statues. We will also bring them before Jesus in the tabernacle and whisper his name. They like to kiss the tabernacle and statues. These simple, beautiful devotions and traditions transmit a deep faith in the child.

In spiritual direction, as they grow older, even at the ages of three or four, they can talk about their faith in very simple terms. Their very simple comments in a spiritual guidance encounter can be profound, and we can tell you that we are often moved at what we hear and learn from our very young children. These spiritual guidance sessions can and should continue indefinitely into the teenage years and adulthood.

The Lord has helped us to foster in our family a healthy mystique for Eucharistic visits amongst our children. It is not uncommon for several of our children to beg to go to a holy hour with mom or dad, or as our four-year-old, Mairead, calls it, "*a holy water*."

Hierarchy of Values

The children will bring spiritual reading with them in proportion to their age, be it scripture or lives of the saints. They spend time praying the rosary, doing their spiritual reading, or praying in silence. The little ones, like our four-year-old, Mairead, might like to sit on a parent's or sibling's lap, or walk around and look at the stained glass or statues, or kneel before the tabernacle, or to pray a decade of the rosary. They might last only about twenty minutes before getting tired or bored. Then, for example, Mairead may be invited to lie down on the pew. She will then sleep in the Lord's presence, which is a beautiful thing in itself.

We try not to be uptight about these things. We want the Eucharistic visits to be natural and pleasant for the children. They have the opportunity to spend time with the Lord as he *radiates* his grace into their souls. They also have some beautiful bonding experiences just being with their parents. The children are profoundly happy at these times, as are we the parents.

Have we ever imposed Mass attendance, Eucharistic visits, or prayer on our children? In a sense, yes, as it is our duty to expose them to these things. But we do it in such a way that they will love these things of God as we do, and will be attracted to them, make them their own, and persevere in them throughout their lives. *If we did not expose our children to experience these things in their younger years so they could get to know them, then how would they come to love them?*

The spiritual life is completely natural to little children. If anything, we simply cultivate what is already there. It is very easy to start this with children when they are very young, before the world has hardened them, making it more difficult once they grow older.

Take, for example, the Sacrament of Reconciliation where we confess our sins to Christ in the person of a priest, and our sins are washed away through the Blood of Christ. While many children are apprehensive about their first confession, our children look forward to it for years. They have witnessed their older siblings and parents going into the confessional on a weekly basis. The little ones can't wait to have the opportunity that they see the rest of the family taking advantage of on a weekly basis with so much naturalness and joy. Then when it is their turn there is no fear whatsoever. It is just a natural progression and a great privilege to begin receiving this sacrament frequently.

Prayer as a family is vital. We need to pray for and with our children from the time they are in the womb. Our children have often prayed by taking holy water and gently blessing the wounds of Christ on a crucifix. They like to kiss his wounds. *This is a deep form of prayer without words.* Prayer does not always need to be expressed in words. *We can learn much from children in the natural ways they pray* when given the opportunity and a little formation.

We have a tradition in our household where often one or two of our children will hold up a crucifix over their heads while the family prays grace before meals. Our babies pick up on this. For example, our daughter Brighde, at age one, often looks for the crucifix before meals. We give her a crucifix and she holds it up above her head while we pray grace. She will then kiss Jesus before handing it back to an older person. She is so proud and joyful to be participating with the family in this prayer and tradition. Before Mass, Brighde, even before age one, would like to go before the altar before Mass and point up to the crucifix above whispering "Jesus". She would genuflect in her own way by squatting down, pat her chest, which is her way of making the sign of the cross, and make little jibber-jabber sounds which is her way of praying.

Our children have often gotten together and conducted *pretend* Masses, where one of our sons would dress up as and fulfill the role of the priest, with other children, including sometimes the parents, taking other roles, such as lector, server, and congregation. They are very good and accurate in reproducing the Mass. Obviously, this is done with everyone's understanding that a real Mass is certainly not occurring, but this tradition demonstrates and further develops a great affinity for the priesthood, and the Mass, the *greatest prayer*.

We have formally consecrated our family to the Immaculate Heart of Mary and to the Sacred Heart of Jesus. This is a devotion we highly recommend. Every day we re-consecrate our lives into the hands of the Blessed Virgin Mary to arrange. *The rosary is our first prayer of choice outside of the Eucharist, and it was our Blessed Mother Mary that led us to Jesus in the Eucharist, to live Eucharistic lives.*

We never miss evening prayer as a family. For us this generally consists of praying briefly to the Holy Spirit, then praying two decades of the rosary, reading and reflecting on a short scripture passage, a short excerpt from another spiritual book, and a silent review of the day in terms of what we did well and where we failed in living God's will that day. We make a firm resolution to try to improve and finish with the Nicene Creed and a few other short prayers. This evening prayer only takes about fifteen minutes, except when dad gets on a roll with his "preaching."

Each of our family members, including parents and children, have a Plan of Life where we essentially identify our root faults and their common manifestations, and make resolutions to live virtue concretely, with God's help, in various areas of our lives such as relates to God, spouse, children, siblings, work, school, social, and service. These are private and are generally only shared with our spiritual directors. They are a great means of making real progress in our human and spiritual formation. We are able to measure and hold ourselves accountable.

We have been given the tremendous grace of being open to vocations to the priesthood, religious, and consecrated life in our family. From the earliest age we form our children to discern, be open to, and to do God's will. This is in actuality quite easy for us as we know that this is what will make a person happy. We want what God wants for ourselves and for our children. Therefore we form our children to trust that they can never outdo God in generosity. They are giving God the first opportunity with their young lives. So far, every one of our children of age has at least attended a summer program to discern whether God wants them to attend a school for formation for the priesthood or consecrated life. Our daughters have done this upon graduation from grade school and our son Shane, after sixth grade. Most of our children have stayed for formation in this environment for an extended period. Time will tell whether or not we will have the honor of having priests or religious in our family, however, we do know that by the grace of God, we are giving him control over our lives.

A religious vocation is something that God has destined for a soul from all eternity. It is very particular to the person. Through the sacraments, prayer, spiritual direction, and through the ordinary circumstances of life, God reveals his plan to the soul. However, it is critical that the person must be immersed as much as possible in an environment in which he is able to hear God's call, and then, especially importantly, he or she must also have the generosity to respond, to act. Our children who have chosen this formation by attending the precandidacy for girls or minor seminary for boys have freely chosen this for themselves. It is not at all imposed. They would not be accepted by the program if it were not their choice in freedom and in love.

Our daughter Grace was attending the precandidacy, and after her first visit home at Thanksgiving, Kathleen wrote a letter to Grace telling her that it would be hard for her to be back at school after the time she spent at home and that she'd probably feel homesick, but to stay close to Christ and lean on him. Grace wrote back to Kathleen telling her, "Mom, don't worry! I already know what God is asking of me, and that is to be here at the precandidacy, and not only that, but to get as many girls as I can to experience it too."

We also know and have experienced that when a child leaves home to discern a vocation, Christ fills the gap. Not only does he fill the gap, but in our case, since sending our eldest to the precandidacy six years ago, and subsequently sending six more to discern their possible vocations to the priesthood or consecrated life, he has blessed us with five more children, three living and two in heaven. Again, God cannot be outdone in generosity.

In summary, our *hierarchy of values* has to be based on God's will and that will must be our *very food*, our sustenance, our driving force, our focus. "My food is to do the will of the one who sent me." (John 4:34) Who ever forgets to eat? Well, we should always have God's will clearly defined and constantly before us in *his* priorities for our lives. We cannot go wrong this way, *God's way*.

He is with us as he was with Shadrach, Meshach, and Abednego, who were willing to be thrown into the fiery furnace rather than worship any false gods, rather than put anything before our Heavenly Father and his will, rather than betray their *hierarchy of values*. But the fire did not touch them. They only felt a cool wind and a dew. *Christ was with them, and he was in control, as he is in command of our lives today and always.* "I can see four men walking about freely in the heart of the fire without coming to any harm, and the fourth looks like a son of the gods." (Daniel 3: 92) Nothing, no harmful fire can touch us when we *live Christ* and his will. We walk freely, we are truly free when we *choose* to live according to God's will for us. We are safe in *Christ's Heart, the definitive burning furnace of Love.*

God's ways and plan for each of us is awe inspiring. He loves us infinitely. We need only be true to his roadmap, and we will be happy in time and in eternity. Be not afraid to *reevaluate* and make *radical changes* for the good, to truly and courageously live by a proper *hierarchy of values*. God is with us!

Chapter 4

Marriage

"They have no wine."
(John 2:4)

Our children will often gleefully exclaim, "Mom and Dad are kissing!" (James) They think it's funny and a bit embarrassing when they observe us demonstrating our love in a chaste embrace and kiss, but we can see clearly that it makes them very happy and secure to see that their parents love and are *in love* with each other. It also helps to make up for the many times that we fall short in charity towards each other.

Although Kathleen and I *do have our quarrels* we are truly one with each other in every way, including spiritually. We are blessed to be on the same page with regard to every essential. This is primarily thanks to the grace of the Sacrament of Marriage and our ongoing consistent sacramental and prayer life.

Kathleen and I have been also been extraordinarily blessed with the outstanding witness of our parents in the way they lived their marriages in charity, dignity, and mutual respect.

In marriage *the husband's ideal is Christ*. He loves his bride like Christ, the Bridegroom, loves the Church, sacrificially, even unto death, death on a cross. He sheds his blood for her.

A wife is virtuous. She is like the moon that so gently reflects the light of the sun, like the Blessed Virgin Mary, who tenderly reflects the light of her Son, Jesus Christ.

"Give way to one another in obedience to Christ. Wives should regard their husbands as they regard the Lord, since as Christ is the head of the Church and saves the whole body, so is a husband the head of his wife; and as the Church submits to Christ, so should wives to their husbands, in everything. Husbands should love their wives just as Christ loved the Church and sacrificed himself for her to make her holy. (Ephesians 5:21-25) "For this reason a man must leave his father and mother and be joined to his wife, and the two will become one body. This mystery has many implications; but I am saying it applies to Christ and the Church." (Ephesians 5:31-32) It would take volumes to begin to cover the depth of the meaning of these scripture passages so we will not try to do so here. Besides, someone already has. Servant of God, *John Paul II* developed a sublime *Theology of the Body* on this theme, which we invite the reader to explore further. An excellent starting point might be Christopher West's, *Theology of the Body for Beginners*.

What is the true essence of marriage? "The marriage covenant, by which a man and a woman form with each other an intimate communion of life and love, has been founded and endowed with its own special laws by the Creator. By its very nature it is ordered to the good of the couple, as well as to the generation and education of children. Christ the Lord raised marriage between the baptized to the dignity of a sacrament." (CCC 1660)

Why do so many marriages fail? In our opinion, one common reason involves false expectations. One or both spouses expect and demand that the other spouse make him or her perfectly happy. *This is a recipe for disaster because we are made for God*, and only God can make us perfectly happy. Therefore, to expect this perfection of a spouse is to make an impossible demand and to set up the marriage for potential failure.

Due to our fallen human nature, ebbs and flows of tension are to be *expected* in a marriage. In fact these *tensions and difficulties are to be embraced.* Marriage is about love, and love can only be truly expressed, love is only authentic, through *sacrifice*. We have to struggle to die to ourselves daily, moment to moment, in each circumstance of our lives as Christ died out of love for the Church.

Rather than expecting marriage to be a fifty-fifty proposition, *each spouse should commit and strive to contribute a hundred percent*, in a sense expecting nothing from the other spouse. What a beautiful thing it is when both spouses take this approach, sacrificing, living by example, *overlooking the defects of the other*. How beautiful a thing it is as well when a spouse continues to give a hundred percent when at least the perception is that the other spouse is not equitably holding up his or her end. This is a very *sublime* thing because it involves even a *greater love*, even a greater sacrifice.

Another deep-seated reason why so many marriages fail today is that they have intentionally rejected openness to the gift of life through contraception, sterilization, and/or abortion. We have addressed this in detail in the *Openness to Life* chapter.

If the reader has made this mistake with respect to openness to life, please don't lose hope. God is infinitely merciful. There remains the opportunity to truly repent, and to begin anew in being open to life through true repentance, which is encouraged for the good of the married couple's souls and their marriage. Most forms of contraception (some of which are abortifacient and really cause a very early abortion) can be easily discontinued, and Natural Family Planning (NFP) substituted. For those marriages where a spouse has been intentionally sterilized, surgical reversal is encouraged where this is possible; and where not possible, the couple is encouraged to make the reparation of saving their marital embrace for the infertile periods, as can be easily learned through a good NFP course and/or book.

Couples that are willing to make reparation and to live openness to life in their marriages will receive not only the many spiritual benefits, but a very practical strengthening of their marriage. We have only touched a very brief summary on this important issue, and encourage the reader to explore this subject further, such as through *The Art of Natural Family Planning*, by John and Sheila Kippley.

Marriage is ordered between man and woman because like God's love, it is called to be fruitful, open to life. "Each of the two sexes is an image of the power and tenderness of God, with equal dignity though in a different way. The union of man and woman in marriage is a way of imitating in the flesh the Creator's generosity and fecundity..." (CCC 2335)

Marriage is indissoluble, committed unto death, like between Jesus Christ and his bride, the Church.

A married couple should *pray together*. Kathleen and I are blessed to pray together daily. We attend daily Mass and make Eucharistic visits and Holy Hours together. We attend the Sacrament of Reconciliation together (of course confessing our sins to Jesus through the priest separately). We pray the rosary together. We attend couple marriage retreats. We often share spiritual insights from our prayer and spiritual reading. We comment to each other on and recommend scripture passages that we feel are timely and appropriate to our current circumstances or spiritual life.

It is astounding to experience the Holy Spirit at work in the way he works through our spouse when we make room for him in our lives and souls. Kathleen and I actually act as each other's spiritual directors. We find ourselves at times essentially giving each other directed meditations. We often cannot wait to share some spiritual insight or light with each other. This is one of the beautiful graces of the Sacrament of Marriage. This is a great joy, and I know we have God to thank for this gift.

If however, as is not uncommon, you and your spouse are not currently on the same page spiritually, accept and love your spouse unconditionally. Don't lament that something is allegedly terribly wrong. See God's providence in this situation. Lead by your witness of charity. Don't harp on your spouse, for example, to hurry up and catch up with where you are supposedly at spiritually. "The unbelieving husband is made one with the saints through his wife, and the unbelieving wife is made one with the saints through her husband." (1 Corinthians 7:14) *Trust* that our Blessed Lord will see to the sanctification of your spouse in his time and way.

I heard somewhere that the most intimate thing a husband and wife can do together, even more than sexual relations, is to pray, and that the idea of this can be frightening especially to men. Essentially I agree with this. All I can suggest is to get past the fears, reservations, and excuses and begin praying together. *If someone told you that there was something you could do for as little as five minutes per day to virtually assure that your marriage would last unto death, wouldn't you do it?* Well this is it! Like anything, once you begin it will become easier.

Marriage is not a couple, but a trinity. The third person is God. We need to allow God to be an integral part of our marriage for it to be healthy. *God is infinitely concerned about our marriages.* It is intriguing that the *first public miracle* Christ performed was at a wedding in Cana. (Cf: John 2) Mary points out, (and she is always attentive to the details) "They have no wine." (John 2:4) Perhaps we could take this to mean, "Jesus, this couple does not yet have you, Jesus, in their marriage. They have no life! They don't have *you*!" So Jesus gets intimately involved. He changes water into wine, a sign of the Eucharist to come. *A couple without Christ is like bland water*. But Christ gives this couple himself. He gives *life* to them and to their marriage. Their marriage now takes on a *transcendent value*, as can ours as well.

"The Eucharist is the very source of Christian marriage. The Eucharistic Sacrifice, in fact, represents

Christ's covenant of love with the Church, sealed with his blood on the Cross. In this sacrifice of the New and Eternal Covenant, Christian spouses encounter the source from which their own marriage covenant flows, is interiorly structured, and continuously renewed. As a re-presentation of Christ's sacrifice of love for the Church, the Eucharist is a fountain of charity." (Familiaris Consortio 57)

What are some practical means for vivifying a marriage? *Program in time to talk*. This is a busy age we live in. We must have a *strong, uncompromising will* in regards to a well-ordered and informed hierarchy of values. We cannot permit lesser important things to overwhelm and eliminate our time to talk with our spouse. We suggest actually scheduling in a time to talk each day for an appropriate period of time, and developing habits along these lines. This could include perhaps time to unwind together with a glass of wine after the children are in bed, or to take a walk together. Learn to listen. Don't try to dominate. Our spouse often just wants to be listened to.

We also recommend having a *date night*, perhaps every week or two, so the husband and wife can get out together alone without the children, for dinner or some other enjoyable activity.

We should greet our spouse with warmth and love, for example when he or she returns home from work, rather than beginning to unload the problems of the day on him or her at that special moment. (Cf: TCM) If the other spouse does need or decide to unload, we should allow this alleviation of tension by listening patiently and helping where possible with a supportive word or action. Humility, charity, and patience are indispensable virtues.

A spouse will never perfect the other by criticizing and pointing out the other's faults. It is best to look in the mirror on a daily basis, and *work on the perpetual plank in one's own eye.* (Cf: Matthew 7:4) For me I usually find a redwood tree there. Betterment of the other spouse will primarily be accomplished through the efficacy of the graces merited *through sacrifice and one's personal example.* That is not to say that one should never charitably correct his or her spouse, but this should be rare, and it needs to be understood that it is not the primary and most effective way of bettering the marriage.

When we fail in charity we should be quick to humbly say we are sorry. Forgive, forgive, and forgive some more. Forgiveness is essential. *Forgive swiftly*, and do your best to *forget offenses*. Nothing good will come from dwelling on and re-living resentment and bitterness over offenses. View thoughts of this nature as you would any temptation toward sin or evil. Reject such thoughts immediately by pushing them out with prayer, by crowding them out by allowing the Holy Spirit to fill you.

We should never abuse the spirit of our family by criticizing or complaining about our spouse to others. We should be *loyal* and defend our family and spouse, *always speaking well of them* and holding them in esteem. Don't hang out your dirty laundry. (Cf: TCM)

Marriage calls for a *delicate charity* and *attention to detail*. It calls for a *profound unity*, an *esprit de corps*. *We should praise our spouse and say, "I love you" often.* We should demonstrate our love with a consistent *special look* or facial expression of love. The *tone of our voice* should also console our spouse with our love and esteem. Our entire demeanor and countenance should exude our love for our spouse. We must learn to acquiesce to the preference of our spouse in the nonessentials. This calls for God's ready help to live all these things consistently. We must pray for and cooperate with this grace.

Marriage calls for *generosity, service, and sacrifice, with constancy.* Very importantly, we should pray for and offer sacrifices on a daily basis for our spouse. *The little daily things are important*, not just the rare, big, epic opportunities. (Cf: TCM) We should never underestimate the graces and help that will be won for our spouse through these means.

Put God first, then your spouse, then your children. If you put God first, your marriage will be fortified beyond your expectations. *To have a strong loving marriage is the best gift a couple can give to their children.* The world itself is in grave need of the witness of strong and beautiful marriages today. It is desperate for this light. We must create a culture that esteems *marriage* and *family*. These words should be whispered with reverence. They are sacred sacraments or signs of God's inestimable love for the world.

Embrace your crosses together. A couple grows closer through carrying the cross together, manifested in the various difficulties, challenges, crises, illnesses of life, even in the death of loved ones. The *cross* is the *enduring super glue* that bonds the spouses together, like two soldiers that have supported each other, suffered, and fought side by side in fulfilling their duty even unto death.

When one spouse is weak, the other should be strong. God is always there to help. There are many graces showered on a married couple through the Sacrament of Marriage. These graces can always be called upon for strength and assistance.

Although both spouses are equal, *the husband is the spiritual head of the family*. He should not be afraid to lead and make decisions. He should be a man of strength but gentleness. He keeps in mind that his wife is the heart, and a head is no good without a heart. *A head without a heart is a <u>dead head</u>*!

A husband praises his wife and reassures her. He protects her from worry. He recognizes her moods and accepts them. He is attentive to detail. He surprises her with flowers and candy even when there is no special occasion. (I must admit that personally I buy my favorite candy as it is commonly understood that the children and I will get to eat most of it. Oh well, it is the thought that counts, right?)

And in your prayer try to often return to the fond and true memory of your spouse w*hen you first met, and on your wedding day.* He or she is still that same loveable person. Perhaps life has presented many challenges you did not expect back then, but you have come through these *together*, and the *providential fire of your tribulations and your love has forged you into the one body you are today, and that is a beautiful thing.* "So then, what God has united, man must not divide." (Mark 10:9-10) Never let anyone or any *inferior* thing tear you and your spouse asunder. God is one with you. He is *love*, your marriage is *love*, and *love endures whatever comes, it does not come to an end.* (Cf: 1 Corinthians) Let's be thankful to God for the gift of our spouses. May we be one with them in time and eternity.

Chapter 5
Motherhood

This is your Mother.
(John 19:27)

A disturbing story occurred when Kathleen was undergoing a caesarean section for delivery of our twins, Maura and Clare (James). Kathleen's regular obstetrician was not available, so the doctor on call delivered the babies. I was in the operating room with her. The doctor had her opened up and in the course of delivering the babies, he turned to me and said that since she was already opened up, he could go ahead and sterilize her by tying her tubes. I guess he was offering an efficient and perhaps discounted two-for-one operation. Of course, I was appalled, shocked and angry at this. I told him that there was no way he was going to do that. I made sure in a very intense and serious way that he understood me. I lost complete trust in him at that time. I kept reminding him that he had better not perform a tubal ligation. He continually assured me that he would not, but I had heard horror stories of doctors thinking they knew better than the patient what was good for her and doing it anyway. Kathleen was, of course, not in much of a position to express her horror and fear at his proposition, but her eyes indicated it to me very clearly. It is utterly appalling that such a proposal was made at all, let alone at such an emotional time. This was vastly inappropriate. As this may be a not so uncommon proposal repeated often to women in this scenario, I dread the real risk that couples might make a bad decision to end their fertility under duress when such a proposal is made to them. Of course, we would never dream of either one of us being sterilized which is so contrary to the truth about the human person and our sexuality, about our sharing in the life-giving and unitive gift of God.

Kathleen had undergone many difficulties with the pregnancy of the twins, so the dominant culture would deceive us into believing that due to this long suffering, her age, number of children, and other factors, we were "entitled" to have her sterilized. This is a lie. Just think, since the twins were born, we have thus far had seven more children, four living and three in heaven. Had this poor, confused doctor had his way, those children and all their descendants, and their eternal souls which were planned and destined by God to live for all eternity, would never have existed.

God has created us to be like him, to be one through him, with him and in him. *God is a giver*. He gives life. He is a life-giver. We are made to be life-givers. Whether blessed with fertility or not, we can all be life-givers spiritually, and through the giving of ourselves.

What a blessing fertility is, to have the love between husband and wife bear fruit in the life of a child brought into the world and into eternity. God is love. All real love entails risk, entails sacrifice. Outside of and unconnected to God there is really no love. If we could only fathom how much Jesus Christ loves givers, risk-takers, those who *pour* out everything they are and have, those who do not reduce their love to economics, finances, and things. Christ loves *extremists*, those who put love before everything else. God is love.

"Jesus was at Bethany in the house of Simon the leper when a woman came to him with an alabaster jar of the most expensive ointment, and poured it on his head as he was at table. When they saw this, the disciples were indignant, 'Why this waste?' they said. 'This could have been sold at a high price and the money given to the poor.' Jesus noticed this. 'Why are you upsetting the woman?' he said to them. 'What she has done for me is one of the good works indeed! I tell you solemnly wherever in all the world this Good News is proclaimed, what she has done will be told also in remembrance of her.'" (Matthew 26:6-13)

You see, God himself defends, protects, and provides for generous souls, "*pourers*", those who don't drip, but *pour* it all out. Christ is so taken by this woman's generosity, of her trust in him, of her willingness to give everything, that he honors her in a special way. He proclaims that her generosity will be told forever. *Mothers are Pourers.*

We are only free, we only conquer fear when we are generous, when we trust completely in God, when we live our lives doing what is in our power, while at the same time, totally dependent on God, completely confident in him, in his love, in his power to bring good out of everything. *He is never outdone in generosity, never!* God is Generosity Incarnate, an Infinite Well of life giving water of generosity.

Mothers are the most beautiful creatures in the world. *There is nothing more beautiful than a mother.* There has never been a beauty pageant winner more beautiful than a pregnant woman. A pregnant woman glows with the grace of God. She is one with God. Her love has borne fruit with the life in her womb. She is transformed into an *other worldly beauty*. Anyone can naturally see this.

  I know, when I see my wife especially when she is pregnant, I experience an overwhelming drive to embrace her. I want to be one with that love that she is exuding. A pregnant woman is a lover, in the true sense of the word. Yes, she is a lover because the love that she gives is very costly to her through the physical difficulties of the pregnancy, through the pain of childbirth, through the mountain of work of mental, emotional, physical, and spiritual self-giving. To be a mother is to be a *pourer* throughout her entire life, unto death, and into eternity. Through all the challenges of motherhood she *owns a deep interior joy*. From the moment she becomes a mother, from the first moment of conception (fertilization), she will never be the same. She is now a *mother*.

  When we hear or utter the name *mother*, really we should bow or genuflect. In a sense, *we are encountering God in a mother*. I dedicate these thoughts and words from the depths of my soul first to the mother of all mothers, the Blessed Virgin Mary, then to my wife, who is a gift from God beyond words, and to both my mother Joan and Kathleen's departed mother Rosemarie (may her soul rest in peace). I further dedicate these thoughts and words to all mothers, to all the mothers who have embraced so many sacrifices and sorrows, selflessly out of love for their children and for the world.

We need to create a culture that honors mothers. We need to honor mothers who are old, wrinkled, perhaps forgotten in nursing homes; to honor mothers whose children perhaps did not seem to turn out as perfectly as their dreams had hoped for. But nothing is lost with God. With God all things are possible.

I am certain that we will find out in eternity that a significant percentage of the population in heaven will have gotten there, in a major part, because of their mothers. Their mothers will have interceded for their children like the Blessed Mother did at the wedding feast at Cana. When the Blessed Virgin Mary told her son Jesus that they had no wine, he gave her what she asked for, for the benefit of the others that she interceded for. (Cf: John 2) Our Blessed Lord never refuses his mother's requests.

I am convinced, without a shadow of a doubt, that he will never refuse any mother when she intercedes for her children. God addresses these words to all of us, but especially to mothers, "Ask and it will be given to you ... what father among you would hand his son a stone when he asked for bread? Or hand him a snake instead of a fish? Or hand him a scorpion if he asks for an egg? If you then, who are evil, know how to give your children what is good, how much more will the Heavenly Father give the Holy Spirit to those who ask him?" (Luke 11:9-13) This goes for her life of giving, praying, and interceding here on earth, as well as when she stands immersed in God at the gates of heaven, with utter confidence that God will grant her that each of her children will enter those gates of paradise. For those mothers who spend themselves worrying and praying for their children, take this one to the bank, your prayers will be answered. Mothers, after a life of spending themselves, will hear the words, "Well done good and faithful servant." (Matthew 25:21), and *they will be heard by God*.

Yes, God gives mothers whatever they ask for their children. Why? Because they are *humble*, they are living signs of humility, and *only the humble are filled with God*. But Christ also gifts mothers with a share of his sorrows and passion to be applied to the salvation of their children. Mothers are other Christs. This applies not only to Christians, but to all people of good will. Yes, we want to share the gift of the Catholic faith with everyone, and it is not an indifferent matter whether those who are offered this gift accept it or not, but everyone is at least indirectly part of the *mystical body of Christ* and can be saved.

Mothers are powerful with God. They are the true definition of tough, and will let nothing stand in the way of the good of their children. No price is too large for a mother. "A woman whose little daughter had an unclean spirit heard about him and straightaway came and fell at his feet. Now the woman was a pagan by birth, a Syrophoenician, and she begged him to cast the devil out of her daughter. And he said to her, 'The children should be fed first because it is not fair to take the children's food and throw it to the house dogs.' But she spoke up: 'Ah, yes sir,' she replied, 'but the house dogs under the table can eat the children's scraps.' And he said to her, 'For saying this you may go home: the devil has gone out of your daughter.' So she went off to her home and found the child lying on a bed and the devil gone."(Mark 7:24-30) What an awesome example of sacrifice, love, *costly humility*, and tenacity of a mother!

The name mother should be whispered with reverence. This story of the Syrophoenician woman is representative of all mothers. There are really no bad mothers, only good mothers, at least amongst those who try, who do their best and persevere regardless of any shortcomings. Yes, we all fall short, but God makes up for this. A mother's life is made up of so many tens of thousands of seemingly ordinary small tasks and sacrifices, but in fact each has an infinite value, when united with Christ. Mothers have a *special dignity* that God has blessed them with. Mothers should be confident in this. Mothers should go through life saying, "*I am a mother; I am fulfilled!* I have no fears or worries because God is with me, and he loves me in an extraordinary way."

Elderly mothers: every wrinkle, gray hair, varicose vein, pain, and frailty you have is a *purple-heart medal* for which you should beam with a holy pride. Mothers, mothers-to-be, grandmothers ... do you hear what I am saying? Do *you realize the grand dignity you have, the necessary sign that you are in the world?*

And we cannot leave out those women who *ache to be mothers*, who have not had this dream fulfilled, or may not be given the grace physically to be mothers. They too should be honored as *mystical mothers*. *God honors the intention and the will*. The *ache* of those women who wish to be mothers but cannot is an *immense gift of sharing in the sorrows of Christ in a redemptive way*. Those aches and sorrows, that pain that cannot be described in words is a *life-giving pain*. It is in itself a real form of motherhood, and motherhood is life-giving. The fruit of this redemptive pain is parceled out to other souls and participates in Christ's redemptive passion for their salvation. This mystical motherhood is not inferior to physical motherhood. It is profound. These mystical mothers will find in eternity that their love and their sorrow bore fruit in many children whom they will be honored by and spend their eternity with in heaven, because it contributed to their salvation.

And we cannot fail to mention the supreme, higher form of motherhood: *spiritual motherhood*, the motherhood of religious and consecrated women, who have wedded themselves to the Bridegroom, Christ. They are mothers to all of us. They have truly surrendered everything, including their natural ache to be physical mothers, out of the ultimate *pouring* out of their souls in living chaste lives through their mystical marriage to Christ. *They are mothers to all of us* in time and eternity. I absolutely believe that if it were not for these consecrated women, these spiritual mothers, in their sacrifices of prayer and service, *the world would not be able to go on existing.* If it were not for their spiritual motherhood, there would not be physical mothers, because the world would long ago have destroyed itself in hate. It is only through the immense infusion of the love of these spiritual mothers that love has been able to prevail. *Love is the most powerful force in the world, more powerful than atomic weapons.* The supreme self-giving of these consecrated women is the *ultimate atomic bomb of love, which radiates through the world*, of which the fallout touches and sustains every person in the world. They have the added efficacy of the *hiddenness* of most of their sacrifices. The largest part of what they give is *hidden*; it is visible only to God, and therefore has a special power to infuse God's love into others. Thank you, God, for our consecrated and religious.

Every baby born is a sign of hope. We all experience this. Even the most hardened person is moved by the sight of a baby. Everyone wants to be in the presence of a baby. Babies are signs of hope in the world, that God has not given up on the human race, that he loves us infinitely. Every new baby born into the world adds a new dimension to that family. Everything is changed. The family cannot imagine itself any longer without that new, unique, unrepeatable person as an integral part. *Every new baby proclaims by his or her existence alone, "God is with us! God is Love!"*

By the grace of God, I started a tradition with our first child of writing a letter of advice for each of my children while they were in the womb. It is only thanks to our Heavenly Father, and their mother, my bride Kathleen, that I have been given these opportunities many times over.

Here are some stories relating to motherhood in our family. When Kathleen was nearing her due date with Mairead, our twelfth living child, one evening she seemed to be in labor with regular contractions so we drove toward the hospital. On the way there, the contractions stopped, and it appeared that she was not actually in labor. I could see that Kathleen was very disappointed.

On the way home we stopped at a Eucharistic adoration chapel. I left her in the car, and told her I was going to stop in and pray for a short time. She did not feel up to going in so she waited there. When I went before Jesus, truly present Body, Blood, Soul and Divinity in the Eucharist in the monstrance on the altar, I knelt down and asked the Lord for a favor. Of course he knows everything, but I shared with him that Kathleen had been suffering much and was ready to have this baby. I asked if he would allow her to go back into labor so we could head back to the hospital.

I ended up praying some more for about fifteen minutes, virtually forgetting that I had made this prayer request (Oh, me of little faith!). When I came back to the car, I found Kathleen in somewhat of a panic. It turned out that shortly after I had gone into the chapel, while she was sitting with a book resting on her pregnant abdomen, her labor began again with such intensity that the first contraction sent the book flying off her stomach and onto the floor. We ended up racing to the hospital due to the renewed intensity of her labor. Beautiful little Mairead was born shortly thereafter. We call her the *Beautiful One*.

As mentioned earlier, our twins were born prematurely at thirty-four weeks. Both ended up in intensive care. Clare recovered quickly and came home after nine days, but Maura ended up in very serious condition with bacterial spinal meningitis and an infection throughout her entire blood system. Medically, there was a high probability of her dying, and we learned that if she survived she would likely have permanent brain damage as well as other organ failure. She had so many transfusions that every vein in her body was blown, except for some veins in her scalp where the remaining IV's and transfusions were eventually administered.

Of course we prayed at her bedside and offered Masses daily, as did many, many of our friends, family, people who heard of Maura's battle for life, and the communion of Saints. We are convinced that God miraculously intervened, for not only did she survive but she has no physical impairment, and has an exceptional intellect. Furthermore, she is one of those children who has a depth and maturity well beyond her age and brings extraordinary joy to her family and everyone she touches.

I recall that when Kathleen was in the hospital on bed rest with the twins, in peril of a dangerously early delivery, I was praying and pacing in front of the house. My attention happened to be drawn to the statue of the Blessed Virgin Mary in front of our home. There was a pot of petunias at the base of the steps there, and two of this plant's stems had grown out horizontally many inches towards the statue in an unusual and extraordinary way, blossoming into two beautiful flowers right by the statue of the Blessed Virgin Mary. These flowers had blossomed closely together, one directly above the other, with the larger flower on the bottom. It turned out that the larger baby, Maura, was the first to be born, perhaps at the bottom of the womb as signified by the flowers. These flowers remained there, blooming beautifully throughout the entire remainder of Kathleen's pregnancy, delivery of the twins, and Maura's extended six-week long hospital stay. To us, it was a sign of hope.

I was given the grace to realize that the Blessed Mother was telling me through this sign that everything was in her hands' and that she would arrange everything to turn out well. You see, we had long ago consecrated our entire family to the Blessed Mother to arrange our lives. She is our advocate and mediatrix of all graces before God, the Blessed Virgin Mary. We know that although we have experienced and likely will have many more difficulties and sorrows in our lives, she is arranging everything for the eternal good of each of our family members. We have offered ourselves through her to Jesus Christ to do with us whatever he will for our own good and for the good of His Mystical Body. This gives us great peace. Not through any merit of our own, but *with Christ, through Mary, we are invincible*, and we know that our lives will bear much fruit.

Chapter 6

Openness to Life

"If Yahweh does not build the house, in vain the masons toil; if Yahweh does not guard the city, in vain the sentries watch.

In vain you get up earlier, and put off going to bed, sweating to make a living, since he provides for his beloved as they sleep.

Sons are a bounty from Yahweh, he rewards with descendants; like the arrows in the hero's hand are the sons you father when young.

Happy the man who has filled his quiver with arrows of this sort; in dispute with his enemies at the gate, he will not be worsted."

(Psalm 127)

We were blessed as a family with the awesome experience of traveling together to Rome for the closing of the Holy Doors at the end of the Jubilee Year 2000 (James). As happens with most pilgrimages, we had great excitement, experiences, and fruits, but it was physically exhausting and difficult. For example, we attended multiple five-hour liturgies in St. Peter's Square where we were packed in like sardines. We were blessed with what we are convinced were real and practical miracles. Not one of our eleven children at the time, nine of whom were girls, ever asked to go to the bathroom. That in itself was a miracle! Even if we had been able to find them a bathroom, we would never have been able to make our way back through the crowds and security to be reunited with the rest of the family. We only realized that we had received this blessing in retrospect, but what a great practical blessing it was!

The following event is humorous, but really a sad commentary on the lack of openness to life so prevalent today in the western world. Unfortunately, the Italians, like most countries of the western world, are well under the population replacement level of an average completed family of 2.1 children. They were fascinated with our family. We had more than one offer to pay us significant sums of money for our baby umbrella stroller, which of course, we were not willing to part with. Many people asked to take a picture of our family.

During the outdoor Masses in St. Peter's Square, we sat in one long row with my wife at one end and me at the other end with the eleven children we had at the time in between us. The Italian women behind and around us would spontaneously reach over to "mother" one of the little ones by tucking her scarf in or putting a blanket around them. Snacks and goodies to the children were offered from all sides as well.

At the end of one of the events in St. Peter's Square, I found myself literally surrounded by a group of women. I didn't initially understand what was going on because of the language barrier. Someone pulled up a chair and motioned for me to get up on it. They began chanting, "Papa Grande! Papa Grande!" meaning "great father". They had obviously been taken in by our large family and were treating me like an anomaly or a rock star. Then someone pulled up another chair and the women took turns getting up on that chair to get their picture taken with me. My family and I thought the matter was hilarious and went along with the photos as kind of a gag.

It was interesting in retrospect to reflect on the fact that the Italian women had paid no attention to my beautiful bride Kathleen, but directed all their adulation toward me. It was as if Kathleen had nothing to do with having all the children. It must be something about the culture that I don't quite understand. I am still trying to live this down with Kathleen.

So, how did we come to currently have nineteen children? As Kathleen explained, I started out being naturally open to having more children after our first since our lives had already changed, and as I naturally loved children. What difference would a few more make? But, this would have never carried us through having the nineteen we are blessed with thus far.

After my reversion to the Catholic faith I began reading about the Church's teaching on life, such as the famous encyclical Letter of Pope Paul VI, *Humanae Vitae (Of Human Life)* and eventually the *Catechism of the Catholic Church*. The Church's teaching on the truth about life and the value and dignity of the human person struck a deep cord in me, thanks to the graces that had been *poured* out upon me through the Sacraments and prayer through no merits of my own.

Thanks to the Church's teachings I came to embrace truths such as the fact that each person is created in God's own image and likeness, that he is unique and unrepeatable, that he has a unique irreplaceable mission from God for the good of the world, and for the salvation of others, that one person's value is in fact greater than the entire created universe as the universe will pass away but the human person is immortal. He will exist for eternity. The human person's eternity will only be beginning when all the stars burn out, as if not even one grain of sand of time in all the oceans of the world has passed.

It is God's hope and intention that each person that comes into existence will exercise his free will to love and serve God and his fellow man and accept his mercy and salvation, so as to be perfectly happy in the bosom of our Father of Mercies for all eternity. God has shared his creative power with us to such an extent that he chooses to depend on our generosity and courage in being open to life to decide whether a particular person he has thought of for all eternity will even come into existence.

I learned beautiful truths about the gift of human sexuality such as "The spouses union achieves the twofold end of marriage: the good of the spouses themselves and the transmission of life." (CCC 2363) and "It is necessary that each and every marriage act remain ordered per se to the procreation of human life." (CCC 2366) I learned that each time a husband and wife engage in the conjugal act it must be both unitive and procreative (open to bringing forth life). Of course, the Church does allow for spouses to space the births of their children for just reasons via the natural means of periodic continence based on self-observation and the use of infertile periods (natural family planning).

Also quoting *Gaudium et Spes*, Paragraph 50 from the Second Vatican Council: "Marriage and conjugal love are by their nature ordained toward the begetting and educating of children. Children are really the supreme gift of marriage and contribute very substantially to the welfare of their parents. The God Himself Who said, 'it is not good for man to be alone' (Gen. 2:18) and 'Who made man from the beginning male and female' (Matt. 19:4), wishing to share with man a certain special participation in his own creative work, blessed male and female, saying: 'Increase and multiply' (Gen. 1:28). Hence, while not making the other purposes of matrimony of less account, the true practice of conjugal love, and the whole meaning of the family life which results from it, have this aim: that the couple be ready with stout hearts to cooperate with the love of the Creator and the Savior. Who through them will enlarge and enrich His own family day by day."

"Sacred Scripture and the Church's traditional practice see in large families a sign of God's blessing and the parents' generosity." (CCC 2373) "Those (couples) merit special mention who with a gallant heart and with wise and common deliberation, undertake to bring up suitably even a relatively large family." (*Gaudium et Spes*, Paragraph 50 Second Vatican Council)

Kathleen and I came to not simply obey a set of laws from an organization, but rather to live the *freedom of love*. God gave us the grace to not only accept all the Church's teachings, but to love them. *The Church is not an institution. The Church is the person of Jesus Christ*, of God himself, of which we make up his *Mystical Body*.

Kathleen and I have met so many people who only needed one word of encouragement or one example to find the courage to do what they already knew they wanted, what God wanted, to be open to having another child in their marriage. Their sense of joy, relief, and peace was evident when they shared or implied their decision to be open to bring another life into time and eternity. No, we are not saying that everyone needs to have as many children as physically possible without regard for their circumstances. But we are encouraging the reader to reevaluate the possibility of having another child if God grants this gift, to reevaluate in a prayerful way open to God's will, with a *supernatural, faith filled perspective*. We are asking the reader not to apply his or her reason/intellect alone, or what the dominant culture says, but also *faith*, and even with a higher regard for faith, so as not to make God small, not to put him in a tiny box. God is with us! He has the power and ability to provide, and He will. There is a great feeling of freedom and peace that one experiences when one steps out in love and trust in our infinitely loving God.

There is an absolute truth, an absolute reality. *God is with us.* He is *always* with us. He is aware of, interested in, and helping us with every single detail of our lives. Furthermore, he is in command. Nothing happens that he does not at least permit. *Although he does not will everything that happens in our lives and in our world, he is so powerful, so mysteriously in command, that he can, and he will bring good out of everything in our lives.* We need to know this. We need to be assured of this, to *live* this.

There is no need to be afraid. Each person's mission is essential, and crucial. But no crucial mission can ever be accomplished without *risk*. *It is only through risk that we can accomplish the great things that God wants of us*, for our good and the good of others. What is holding us back? Why all this confusion and fear? God is with us. Yes, he truly is!

One of my favorite gospels, one of my favorite reality checks, is in the Gospel according to *Mark 4:35-41*. It is the story about the disciples crossing the lake with Jesus asleep in the stern. "On that day, as evening drew on, Jesus said to his disciples, 'Let us cross over to the other side.'" Yes, he wants us all to cross to the other side. But, there is a risk involved. There is a mystery involved. Perhaps it is evening; perhaps it is late. Maybe we are tired, but he wants us to cross to the other side.

"And leaving the crowd behind, they took him, just as he was in the boat." Yes, leaving the crowd. Leaving the opinion polls, political correctness, the dominant culture, the culture that says one or two children should be enough, acquire more things and you will be happy; the culture that *insanely* makes a god, an idol, a savior, a religion, an obsession out of *politics*; the dominant culture that says it's all about power, prestige, early retirement, spending your final years playing golf, taking it easy, and *waiting to die. Then what?*

We tend to want to be in control. We want all our ducks to be in a row before we venture out to give God what He wants in our lives. "Lord, let us win the lottery first!" "Let us have all our finances locked in to supposedly be secure that our current children and our possible next child have their private college education fully paid for, and then we will be open to life." Certainly we can apply prudence in our lives where prudence belongs, but what is often lacking in today's western culture is *faith*, and *faith entails risk*.

Surrendering our comfort zone to our Blessed Lord includes pain and purification, but for our good. We can not reduce the value of a human life to an illusory sense of control and assurance that we will be able to provide that child a college education and all the "things" we *think* he needs to be happy and fulfilled.

After all, we do not co-create with God persons who will be totally dependent and useless consumers. No, every person comes into the world with unique gifts to contribute for his own good and for the good of others, and that includes every person, even those with so-called disabilities and illnesses. It is supreme arrogance and lunacy to think that we parents alone somehow possess our children, and are responsible for them on our own. We must give God his infinite due!

God wants to reach us with his truth and encouragement, even through examples that nature provides around us. What if the majestic trees of the forest were to say, "let us grow in greenhouses as potted plants where we will be safe and comfortable?" They would never mature. Their potential, their mission would never be fulfilled. No, they *risk* to let their seeds fall where they will and die. Those seeds then take root in the earth where there is dirt, vermin, death, pain, and darkness. Eventually the trees sprout up and reach up for the sun, to the life-giving sun and to the heavens. In order to reach for the sun, there must be a willingness to embrace the inescapable risks and challenges; and while they are reaching up and developing their full potential, fierce storms are mixed in with the sunny tranquil days.

Life is tremendously short. We need to step out and make the most of it. God is asking us to be generous in some way according to our possibilities. What is he asking of you? For many could he be asking your openness to having another child, if he so blesses you?

You don't have to have fourteen today. Our Blessed Lord is just asking us to be open, to trust, to be open to having perhaps one more child for now, to make the best of the circumstances and opportunities he is blessing us with today; then to discern the possibility of having yet another child down the road, but *never to shut God out of our decision making process, to never definitively marginalize his will*. We must always be open to his will. He does not want us to be *potted plants*.

"They took him, just as he was." We need to take Jesus with us. We need to be with the Lord, and we need to take Jesus just as he is, the Jesus who loves us, the Jesus who is Mercy incarnate; and the Jesus who is demanding, who wants the best for us, who wants us to live life to the fullest without fear. Our Blessed Lord wants us to put him first, to be open to the children he wants to bless us with, to put him and our families above things, above power, above prestige.

"There were other boats with them." And when we strive to fulfill our mission and gallantly venture out, putting God and his will first, others will be invigorated and emboldened. They will look to our example and find courage to take a risk themselves, to leave fear behind, and to begin to live their lives to the full.

"Then it began to blow a gale and the waves were breaking into the boat." Sure, it can seem difficult to take risks, to do God's will, to be open to having a large family, to die to ourselves, to put our spouse and children before our own pleasure, things, and fears. But these are all opportunities to grow in faith, to grow in love, to *exercise our spiritual muscles*. None of us live selflessness perfectly, and Kathleen and I unquestionably don't; but God wants us to *give our best effort* each day, even though we fall short. *The growth and merit is in the effort and struggle. How could we ever love if there were no opportunities for difficulty or sacrifice?* This is God's work. He is always there to help us.

"But he was in the stern, his head on the cushion, asleep." Sometimes when we follow the Lord and make an effort to do his will it will seem like he is not there, as if he has abandoned us, left us to ourselves, as if he is unaware of our dire situation. But the truth is, he is always there, aware of and *supremely interested in every detail of our lives*, always caring, and always in absolute command, *even when he is asleep*. Archbishop

Luis Martinez wrote a beautiful, extensive meditation on this very gospel passage. It has been printed in English under the title *When Jesus Sleeps*. It is a beautiful book, a beautiful meditation.

"Master, do you not care? We are going down!" Yes, he cares, but he permits situations in our lives that take us out of our comfort zones. These are opportunities for us to grow in love, faith, hope, and virtue; to be transformed more into Christ. God is our infinitely loving Father. A good parent will not continue to hold his child's hand to cross the street as the child grows into his teens, twenties, thirties, and forties. A good parent knows when it is time to encourage the child to venture forth on his own.

When a parent teaches his child to swim, will the child not complain, "Don't let go. I'm afraid! I'll drown!" But, the parent helps and encourages the child to take the risk, and when the child discovers he can stay above water through his trepid, but gallant efforts, he is proud as can be! All along the parent was there to save the child if he went under, although the child could not perhaps perceive it at the time, being so preoccupied with his fears, challenges, and efforts at hand. The child would never develop, never mature, never be capable of any grand accomplishments unless the parent permitted him to take risks, to step out of his comfort zone, his *bubble*, to accomplish something.

Our Heavenly Father is like this with us because he loves us, and is willing to do what is best for us regardless of our protests, thanks be to God. If it was up to us we would stay forever in our comfort zone, but *God loves us too much for that; so he is always encouraging us through providential circumstances, events, and people in our lives to trust him more, to take risks, to accept, and embrace difficulties and even tragedies in our lives, so we can grow and mature, and make the most of our lives.*

"And he woke up and rebuked the wind, and said to the sea, 'Quiet now! Be calm!' And the wind dropped and all was calm again." Yes, the Lord, with a word can quiet a storm on a lake. And if we permit him, he can calm the worst storm, the *Category 5 Hurricane that rages in our interior when we don't have Christ in the boat of our soul*. Do you think there are storms in your life that are currently raging or yet to come that are beyond our blessed Lord's power? *Be convinced, there is nothing that will ever happen or can ever happen that is beyond the power and control of our loving and merciful God*. Listen, we are *invincible* when we take Jesus into our boat. *Nothing can harm us when Christ is in our boat, nothing! Don't doubt*. Count on this!

"Then he said to them, 'Why are you so frightened? How is it that you have no faith?'" Why do we not yet have faith, *a real faith that is relevant to our daily lives*? Why not yet? Why don't we sufficiently trust and believe in God? If we take the time to reflect, we will see the innumerable times that our merciful Father has cared for and protected us. We only need a little *supernatural eyesight* that is enhanced through prayer, and for Catholics the sacraments, in order to be able to grasp this reality. How many times does our Blessed Lord have to intervene for us, to provide for us, to show his love for us, before we will stop the *interior storm of being terrified*, before we will truly have faith, a living deep faith that continuously permeates every aspect of our lives?

We need to ask God, to give him permission to bequest us with an *unshakeable faith*. This is God's work, *but we must offer him our consent,* and cooperate with his graces. When much is given, much is expected. With this kind of faith built on rock, we are capable of living our mission in life to the full for our good and the good of others. *We leave impotent mediocrity behind.* What a *magnificent adventure* our life becomes when we leave fear behind and have faith.

"They were filled with awe and said to one another, 'Who can this be? Even the wind and the sea obey him.'" Who is this? It is Jesus, our Lord, our Creator, our Savior, and he is in command. He knows what will become of us. He always wants our good, and will always arrange things for our benefit.

There is really only one power that can stand in the way of God's will. What is that power? What could we say is the power that is virtually equal to God himself? It is the power of a gift he has given us. This is an awesome, but fearsome power. And it is so powerful because it is so absolute. It is absolute because God himself has given it to us and he will never revoke his gifts. He is faithful and true. (Cf: Revelation 19: 1) And this gift, that will never be revoked, this gift that is so awesome and fearsome, is the gift of our *free will*.

This is why we must pray, and pray some more, for the grace of God's help to exercise this power, this *free will* in accordance with Almighty God's will. His will is always for our good and the good of others. And in order to exercise our free will in line with God's transcendent will, we must be a courageous, faith filled, grace filled people. Really the safest way, the most efficacious way, to exercise this awesome and fearsome gift of free will is to *surrender and abandon ourselves to God's most holy will.* Then God will providentially, lovingly rattle us out of our confusion and fear. He will empower us to take risks for the good. He will give us his *supernatural vision* to fall in line with his perfect hierarchy of values, to put God and his things first, then our spouse, then our children, then our work and service. We have to die to our old selves and to be risen with Christ so we can *live Christ*. (Cf: Philippians 1:21)

Kathleen and I have many times been challenged about the size of our family by people, even by relatives, who are often concerned and mean the best. One of the greatest means of persuasion to help them understand that our choice to have a large family was right and good and in accordance with God's will is to take out a picture of our complete family, or to point the children out if they are near by. Then I will ask which of these children should have been our last? Where should we have stopped? Which of these children should not have been born? Which of these children do you think has been brought into existence in opposition to God's will? I will ask this in a charitable tone.

Although I have seldom, if ever, experienced the person who has challenged the size of my family declare that they were wrong, and that they were now in full agreement with our radical openness to life and trust in God, I believe my challenging premise does put things into perspective and cause the person to reflect more deeply on the subject.

I have yet to have someone answer this question by maintaining that Kathleen and I should have stopped at a particular child. This has never happened because of the grave reality that such a response would imply. By virtue of their failure to answer this question by selecting particular beautiful and unique children to have never existed, implies that the challenge to our family's size does not hold merit. To select a point at which we should have ceased the prayerful discernment and living of God's will in regard to openness to life in our marriage, would be to imply that the children born after that point would have been better off not existing, and that the world is better off without them. How could anyone sincerely and in good conscience make such a statement?

The whole idea of overpopulation is a myth. Anyone who has flown in a plane or taken a drive in the country can clearly see that densely populated areas are minuscule compared to the vast, open, sparsely inhabited land. Look at the grave damage done to so many countries, especially in the western world, where the average completed family size is well below the replacement rate of 2.1 children. There are grave societal and economic consequences of this. The consequences being currently experienced are only the tip of the iceberg compared with those potentially to come. One example is the growing percentage of elderly compared to younger working adults. There is an ever increasing motive to attempt to rationalize euthanasia. The prevalent *culture of death*, the abortion and contraception mentality, breeds more and more selfishness and self-centeredness in the individual and in society, which results in increased *fear*. This is a volatile and disordered recipe for evils such as abortion, euthanasia, and wars to flourish.

When a culture pushes God's gifts and his will aside, it pushes God aside. When we are left to ourselves, we encounter disaster. God does not impose himself on us as he completely respects our free will, but we are made free in order to choose to do what we ought, to choose God and his will and truth. *We cannot remain locked up in our fears and self-centeredness and expect to live happy and fulfilled lives.* Although it can seem challenging and difficult to trust God, to take risks, to step out of our comfort zone, to do God's will, this is what truly brings us happiness, fulfillment, and peace.

We recognize that many parents who are trying very hard complain that they are struggling with perhaps one, two, or three young children, and are therefore concerned about having another. We have nothing but compassion and love for them in their struggles and concerns. But we want what is best for them, and we like to encourage these parents with the reality check that their young children will not always be little. The little ones do grow and become more mature, becoming more capable of helping around the house and with the new little ones to come. God really has thought all these things out in his great and generous plan for life. We have found also that as we have grown older, having less energy than when we were younger, God has blessed us with older children now who can appreciably help with responsibilities around the house and with the children.

On a lighter note, (*perhaps the reader at this point is saying that it is about time*) barely an acquaintance from church once told Kathleen that when she falls asleep at night, instead of counting sheep, she tries to name all the Littleton children in order.

How did we end up having nineteen children? Well I can assure you of one thing. We never would have had this many if it were not for the gift of our faith in God, a God who always provides what is truly necessary, a God who tells us not to worry: "Set your hearts on his kingdom first and on his righteousness, and all these other things will be given you as well. So don't worry about tomorrow: tomorrow will take care of itself. Each day has enough trouble of its own." (Matthew 6:16) Kathleen and I are the first to say that it seems to be a *practical impossibility* to have and to raise fourteen living children in this day and age; *but in all ages God never changes* and he tells us, he tells every age, he tells *you* the same thing he told the Blessed Virgin Mary through the angel Gabriel in her impossible situation: *"Nothing is impossible to God"*. (Luke 1:37) We must believe this. We need to be convinced, unwavering. God does not lie. He is *the Truth*. He is in command of every detail of our lives, he is with us, and he who is *Generosity Itself*, will never be outdone in generosity. *Trust him!*

Photographs

All sixteen of us July 2006

The flowers by Our Lady - to us a little sign of hope for our premature twins

PHOTOGRAPHS

Our wedding day August 6, 1983

Jim and his six valentines 1995

Jim and his two daughters 1987

PHOTOGRAPHS

The twins reunited with the family at last, making an even ten October 1997

First day of school 2000

Always the proud papa with #14 2006

Photographs

Shannon and Grace at 19th century ball 2006

Kathleen and her babies May 2006

PHOTOGRAPHS

Jim with his fisher girls 2005

Summer fun 2004

PHOTOGRAPHS

Big girls with little girls May 2006

Irish all the way March 2002

PHOTOGRAPHS

The wonder of a newborn - Mairead with Shealagh 2006

Colleen and Shane "play" Mass - May 1999

The healthy and holy twins on First Communion Day
April 2005

PHOTOGRAPHS

Our family of fourteen "on stage" at a Youth and Family Encounter July 2003

Chapter 7

Miscarriage

"I am the resurrection. If anyone believes in me, even though he dies he will live, and whoever lives and believes in me will never die. Do you believe this?"
(John 11:26)

I (James) remember Kathleen and I having the beautiful, but sorrowful experience of holding our perfectly formed stillborn son James Paul, miscarried at four-and-one-half months gestation. Here, we were given the blessing of a dim understanding of the immense, unfathomable ache the Sorrowful Virgin Mary must have felt when she held the lifeless body of her son, Lord and Savior, Jesus, in her blessed arms. The umbilical cord was wrapped and twisted tightly many times around James Paul's tiny neck, cutting his life here on earth very short, but commencing his eternity and mission in heaven.

After I visited Kathleen in the hospital the next day, the nurse suggested to Kathleen after I left that I should seek professional psychiatric assistance.

(Perhaps by now, in the process of reading this book, the reader is in agreement with this nurse.) When Kathleen asked why, she said that it was due to my not appearing devastated. She assessed that I must be suppressing all my feelings, and that I was therefore in a psychologically dangerous condition of denial. The nurse was unable to comprehend that although we loved James Paul deeply, and were experiencing the profound sorrow of missing him, we had *faith,* and did not see death on earth as the end.

Per the *Catechism of the Catholic Church*: "The obedience of Jesus has transformed the curse of death into a blessing." (CCC 1009) "For those who die in Christ's grace it is a participation in the death of the Lord, so that they can also share in his Resurrection." (CCC 1006) So although we mourned our son's death we are filled with our hope and confidence in his resurrection.

As mentioned in the Chapter, *How We Came to be a Family*, we named each of our miscarried children. Where possible, we baptized them, had funeral services and buried their bodily remains in a Catholic cemetery. We had providentially named our fourth miscarried child, Frances Xavier, after the famous American saint,

MISCARRIAGE

Frances Xavier Cabrini. There is a designated infant section for babies' burial plots at this cemetery where we buried her. It was only after our baby was named and buried, when visiting her grave for the initial time, that to my great consolation I first noticed a statue of a certain saint approximately fifty-feet away overlooking Frances Xavier's grave. This statue depicts the saint embracing a child. And who is the saint? You guessed it. *St. Frances Xavier Cabrini*! I know our little one is being well looked after in the communion of saints.

I am greatly consoled by the Church's teaching on the *Mystical Body of Christ*. All those in heaven, purgatory, and on earth make up our Blessed Lord's *Mystical Body*. Christ is our Head. To paraphrase an insight from Servant of God, Archbishop Fulton J. Sheen, *when St. Paul was knocked off his horse he was asked by Jesus, "Why are you persecuting me?"* (Acts 9:4) *Me? Why did he say me? Christ had risen from the dead, ascended into heaven, and was seated at the right hand of the Father. How could he be persecuted? By "me", Jesus was referring to the members of his Mystical Body.* (Cf: *Your Life is Worth Living*, page 127)

I am convinced that our five miscarried children are just as real, just as alive, just as immortal, and unrepeatable as my living children on earth. They were each made in God's image and likeness from the moment of conception. Our Merciful Father has thought of them with infinite love from all eternity. Life as we know it on earth is short. Eternity is forever. We pray and believe that our miscarried children are already living their eternity in heaven, in the presence of God, perfectly fulfilled and happy. "As regards children who have died without Baptism, the Church can only entrust them to the mercy of God, as she does in her funeral rites for them. Indeed the great mercy of God who desires that all men should be saved, and Jesus' tenderness toward children which causes him to say: 'Let the children come to me, do not hinder them,' allows us to hope that there is a way of salvation for children who have died without Baptism." (CCC 1261)

We believe that when one suffers a miscarriage, all reasonable efforts should be made to recover the baby for baptism where appropriate and possible, and burial. This may require the parents being, with the help of God, convinced, focused, insistent, and unwavering with the medical institution and personnel if the miscarriage occurs at a hospital. We have undergone this experience at the hospital, as well as the experience of recovering our baby's tiny, but just as real, human, and dignified remains at home after a miscarriage. For Christians, baptism should be administered if there is *any* possibility that the infant is still alive short of obvious decomposition, as the sacramental rite of baptism can only be administered to the living. If clergy is not present the parents then can baptize their child. "In case of necessity, any person can baptize provided that he have the intention of doing that which the Church does and provided that he pours water on the candidate's head while saying: 'I baptize you in the name of the Father, and of the Son, and of the Holy Spirit." (CCC 1284)

If the infant is clearly deceased, although one cannot perform a sacramental baptismal rite, the body should be treated with delicate dignity and the child given a proper burial. "The bodies of the dead must be treated with respect and charity, in faith and hope of the Resurrection. The burial of the dead is a corporal work of mercy; it honors the children of God, who are temples of the Holy Spirit." (CCC 2300)

Sometimes it is not physically possible to obtain the baby's remains, such as when a miscarriage occurs at a very early stage and the baby's remains are not noticed or able to be found at the time of the event. Or, perhaps, such as in our case with our first miscarried child, one did not know or think of these teachings. In those cases, *nothing is lost*. We would encourage the parents to simply pray and desire the *mystical baptism* of that child, and *be hope-filled and confident in God's mercy* in granting salvation in his way to the child. *It is never too late with God.*

I am convinced that God permits our miscarried children in a mysterious but real way to hear our prayers, and to be one with our family. I am certain that we have a *team of saints in heaven* watching over and interceding for our family, and *for the world*. I am further convinced that I will retain the mark of their father, as will Kathleen retain the mark of their mother, as will their brothers and sisters retain the mark of being their siblings for all eternity.

Therefore Kathleen and I continue to exercise our role as their parents by giving them responsibilities, missions in heaven through our prayer. "The witnesses who have preceded us into the kingdom, especially those whom the Church recognizes as saints, share in the living tradition of prayer by the example of their lives, the transmission of their writings, and their prayer today. They contemplate God, praise him, and constantly care for those whom they have left on earth. When they entered into the joy of their Master, they were 'put in charge of many things'. Their intercession is their most exalted service to God's plan. We can and should ask them to intercede for us and for the whole world." (CCC 2683)

For example, we have given our miscarried children in heaven specific missions such as the hope of this book reaching as many persons as possible to help them in some way in accordance with God's will. So since you are reading this book, their intercessory prayer has paid off in your life, as well as in everyone you may effect with any positive impact this book may have on your life, by the grace of God.

We have given our miscarried children other projects as well, including interceding for the needs of and the overall sanctification of our family, for an end to abortion, for the success of a particular school, and for vocations to the priesthood and consecrated life in the Church.

Although their life on earth has ended, our deceased children are continuing to fulfill their mission in heaven. I am absolutely certain that they have received and accepted this request, and are in fact interceding with all their might before Almighty God to accomplish their mission.

Of course the prerogative of having an ongoing, productive, and deep relationship with one's deceased children does not apply only to our family. *It is available to everyone.*

I also believe I am able to commune with my children at any time by simply entering my own heart in prayer. Since I am God's own temple, as he made me such in a mystical way through no merit of my own, and since God is present in my heart, then mystically, so are my children able to be, in a sense, present in my heart where I meet them in prayer, because they and I are one with Christ, incorporated into his Mystical Body.

"Heaven is the blessed community of all who are perfectly incorporated into Christ." (CCC 1026) If God is in heaven, and since heaven is heaven because God is there, then in a mystical, but real sense, heaven is present. It has already begun in my heart, because God resides there. My children and I can therefore communicate in Christ through prayer of the heart. I am convinced of this. "To live in heaven is to 'be with Christ.' The elect live 'in Christ,' but they retain, or rather find their true identity, their own name." (CCC 1025)

I do want to make the clarification that I am not trying to reduce or encapsulate heaven into the tiny, faint facet of my comments above. "This mystery of blessed communion with God and all who are in Christ is beyond all understanding and description." (CCC 1027)

I am also not claiming that I hear voices, but I am confident that God has the power to, and does permit my children to be aware of my prayers pertaining to them, and that I can count on their response. In any case, the most profound means of communication between those that love each other is in *silence*, through being contentedly aware of and enjoying each other's presence. We are beyond doubt one in the *Mystical Body* of Jesus.

I commune with my children in another *most profound way at every Mass*. "The Eucharist is the memorial of Christ's Passover, that is, of the work of salvation accomplished by the life, death, and resurrection of Christ, a work made present by the liturgical action." (CCC 1409) My deceased children are there, at, and incorporated in the Mass with me. "To the offering of Christ are united not only the members still here on earth, but also those already in the glory of heaven." (CCC 1370)

In a mystical reality the entire *Mystical Body* of Christ, including those living on earth, those in purgatory, and those in heaven are unified, involved, and incorporated into, and made one in the host, which in the Mass, becomes the true and *real* Body, Blood, Soul and Divinity of Jesus Christ. "The whole Church is united with the offering and intercession of Christ." (CCC 1369) We are all one, unified in the infinite love of God. I not only do and can communicate with my children at every Mass, remembering each by name, but I am really and truly one *with* them. This, of course is only one of an infinite number of treasures, mysteries, and blessings the Eucharist holds for us, because *in the Eucharist we encounter God himself*.

"The unity of the Mystical Body: the Eucharist makes the Church. Those who receive the Eucharist are united more closely to Christ. Through it Christ unites them to all the faithful in one body – the Church." (CCC 1396)

"The Eucharistic sacrifice is also offered for the faithful departed who have 'died in Christ but are not yet wholly purified,' so that they may be able to enter into the light and peace of Christ." (CCC 1371)

We are united in the *Mystical Body* of Christ. *Nothing is ever lost with God. Everything is always made new and better by him.* God is a lover, a giver. He is with us always. We have nothing to fear. *When we have our Blessed Lord, we have everything.* We need to know this and to live this. He is with us, he is in command of every detail of our lives, he loves us infinitely, and we should *not be afraid*.

We who have family members that have died in the grace of God, we who have faith, look forward with unshakeable hope, confidence, and anticipation of being reunited with our loved ones in heaven with our infinitely loving God for all eternity. Imagine the profound experience, once the veil is lifted, of meeting our deceased child, relative, or friend that perhaps died at eight weeks in the womb, or in a deteriorated state at an advanced age; and to greet this loved one in a resurrected body, perhaps with the appearance of a thirty-year-young, perfected, transfigured body and spirit, one in the love of Christ. *We will then see and know how our Father of Mercies really was able to and did bring good out of everything in our lives and deaths.*

Maximilian Mary, Theresa Gerard, James Paul, Frances Xavier and Joseph Faustina: your mom, your dad and your brothers and sisters love you. Pray for us! We will talk later today in our hearts in prayer. We will be with you tomorrow at Mass. And through the mercy of Jesus, we *will see you in heaven* with the Lord for eternity.

Chapter 8

Formation of Children

It is all God's work.

(2 Corinthians 5:18)

The D'ya Understand Me Story: We were driving along in our extended fifteen-passenger van with the whole family (James). The younger children were being very rambunctious, making a lot of racket, and getting on my already frayed nerves as I was driving. I blew my stack, and shouted for everyone to be quiet. I regressed into my south side Irish way of speaking, and capped off my admonishment with "D'ya understand me!" in a loud gravelly yell. There ensued a complete shocked silence in the van for about ten seconds. Then out of the depths of the back of the van came the five-year-old voice of my son, Patrick, perfectly imitating me: "D'ya understand me!" Everyone cracked up laughing. Then all of the kids made repeated impersonations, "D'ya understand me!" keeping us in stitches. Still to this day this impersonation is making the rounds in our family and never fails to produce some laughs.

With regard to formation of children, with all mathematical certainty, *the will of the parents must exceed the total combined will of the children, and with constancy and consistency.* Many times I've said to my children, *"Can you move a brick wall with a squirt gun?"*

Youth are uniquely idealistic. They are full of energy and natural zeal. These gifts and strengths must be channeled towards the good however.

Before offering any advice with regard to the formation of youth, we need to make some clarifications. "The spirit is willing but the flesh is weak." (Matthew 26:41) Kathleen and I are far from perfect parents. I will speak for myself by saying that I know from experience how very weak the flesh is. One of my principle faults is that of impatience. I make grand resolutions on a daily basis to be patient, serene, encouraging, and to be a good example for my children; yet every day I fall short to a greater or lesser degree. At times the grind from the pressures and reality of providing for and raising a large family can seem to be overwhelming. I often suffer from anxiety, irritability, and falling short in charity.

Having owned up to this, however, by the grace of God, we resolve never to be discouraged. Our compassionate Father in heaven knows how we are; he knows our faults. Our Lord Jesus Christ, the Father's only Son, experienced human weakness himself. Even he felt overwhelmed as described in his agony in the garden in scripture. Yes, life can be difficult, even overwhelming, but Jesus Christ gives us the prescription for this. He tells us that we should be awake and praying. (Cf: Matthew 26:41) In other words, we must be people who are tuned into God. God is with us! We must be believers. We have to ask for and accept his help constantly. This is where we find the strength to forge ahead. Not that we advance perfectly, but *the merit is in the struggle.*

How did Christ overcome his great distress in the garden? *With prayer!* With prayer he was able to forge forward in his mission, to even embrace death and the *pouring* out of every last drop of blood and water in his body. But it did not end there, as it does not end there for us. He rose from the dead. He made all things new. Our lives are merely a series of small Good Fridays and Easters, small crucifixions, deaths, and resurrections, culminated in a final death, judgment, and resurrection when our time on earth comes to a conclusion. We do not know when that moment and day will be but in the meantime we must bear fruit with this great gift of time and talents God has entrusted to us.

We have to be very careful not to place a disordered, undue pressure on ourselves to be perfect parents raising perfect children. This would be to base our efforts and goals on the impossible. This is a recipe for despondency and failure. No, we are called to *struggle* towards perfection for ourselves and for our children. The merit is in the struggle, in the effort. The perfection itself lies in the endeavor, in the fight, in trusting in Almighty God, that he is with us to help us, and that he unconditionally loves us.

We have to recognize and accept our human shortcomings, and strive forward to produce grand fruit with our lives regardless. God's grace is much bigger than our faults. He merely needs our faith, trust, and efforts, and he will accomplish great things through us. "There is nothing I cannot master with the help of the one who gives me strength." (Philippians 4:13-14)

Yes, we are weak, the flesh is weak, but Christ said to St. Paul, "My grace is enough for you. My power is at its best in weakness." (2 Corinthians 12:9) So, in spite of our weaknesses and shortcomings, we refuse to give into the temptation to be discouraged, to quit. *In writing this book, we refuse to acquiesce to the temptation that since we fall short as parents we should not bother giving advice.* Listen, if we waited until we were perfect before we tried to do something good for God and others, we would never accomplish anything. So here goes with some advice and examples from me, Kathleen, and our family. Our hope is that at least some points will resonate with you the reader so that you will find some help, encouragement, and consolation.

Kathleen and I believe that our children should be showered with unconditional love and have the certitude that they are in fact loved by their parents, but that at the same time we must be demanding of them. We are trying to lead by example, because true love is total self-giving, not just receiving. We raise our children with a *spirit of sacrifice*, and so we cannot be afraid to demand sacrifice from our children.

We do not want our children to come to us when they are grown and say, "Mom, Dad, why did you ruin me by always giving in? Why didn't you challenge me? Why did you always give in when I complained? Why did you always give me what I wanted, when I wanted it? Why didn't you give me the capacity for sacrifice? Why didn't you form my will when you had the chance?"

We try to form our children to be obedient. *Obedience is expected to be immediate and joyful, manifesting quality and diligence.* In other words, when they are asked to do something, they are expected to do so immediately with a positive attitude, giving their best to the details of the task, and getting it done as quickly as is reasonably possible, without wasting time. The lack of any one or more of these qualities is really not obedience.

For example, if the requested task is done with a bad attitude, the peace is disturbed. If the job is done poorly, or the task is drawn out due to lack of commitment, disorder results. We do not accept complaints when giving an instruction to one of our children. A complaint will generally double a chore.

The children are, of course, ingenious in getting around rules. For example, I may ask a child to do a particular chore and the child will respond by saying that he or she has a question, but that it is really not a complaint. However, there is generally an actual complaint disguised within the question. So I often remind my children that although they may ask a question about the directive, the question may be construed as a complaint, which will result in consequences. Generally the child will then decline to ask the question.

We have a saying that "*apostrophe 't' words*" are bad words," and that they should not be used. "*Apostrophe 't' words*" include the following: "don't, won't, can't, couldn't". Rather we Littletons say, "do, can, will." We are "*conquerors*". The main enemy we conquer is immensely powerful and fearsome. Our archenemy has a three-letter name, and that name is *ego*. We do battle and conquer our egos with God's help along with our efforts.

Kathleen and I try to present authority and strength tempered with love, motivation, and regular signs of affection. By the grace of God, we are a family that profusely shows love to each other with hugs and kisses. This was not the custom in the families Kathleen and I grew up in, but we have developed it nonetheless. We have had the blessing to see the fruit of our older teenage daughters often walking arm-in-arm due to the unabashed esteem, affection, and closeness they have with one another.

I have been given the great grace of being able to get any one of my children to smile or laugh within five seconds no matter how irritated or upset the child may be. That is with one exception. Our daughter, Bridget, whom we call "*The Great,*" is able to hold a straight face with her father. Everyone else, and this has been proven hundreds and hundreds, perhaps thousands of times, will without fail smile or laugh within five seconds. This works just as well with the teenagers. To achieve this, I merely look at the child with a certain sly look and challenge him or her to look me in the eye, proclaiming with infallible confidence that he or she will smile within five seconds. I do this with absolute assurance that I will succeed, as I always do (except with Bridget). Once the child makes eye contact, I begin to count. Generally by the time I have said "one," the child is laughing. Often the child is laughing before I begin to count. There is something about the challenge and the power of suggestion, but it works every time.

In terms of discipline, sometimes one child will report an infraction that another child has committed against him or her, and I will bring both of them together and ask the offended one whether I should punish, or have mercy. I leave it to the offended one to decide. Often when the offended one chooses mercy for the offender, I will decide not to impose a punishment. I believe that the lesson of mercy and forgiveness for both will teach a far greater lesson than any punishment. On a rare occasion the offended one chooses punishment instead of mercy, and I will ask that he or she consider things more deeply thinking about the times they have been shown mercy by God, myself, and others, before making their decision. Usually this does the trick, although admittedly not always.

We try predominantly to use positive encouragement and motivation to form our children. Of course, we also utilize punishment as a consequence of unacceptable behavior. The punishments vary, and often need to fit the particular child. For younger children we may use a time out, or going to bed for a period of time, or perhaps a controlled, balanced, corporal punishment. At times we will have a child write an essay on a virtue or perhaps write an apology including ten positive qualities they see in the child they were angry or in a dispute with. We might have the child write fifty times, "I will be charitable." Writing something simple and mechanical like this tends to work better for the younger children, who will otherwise spend an inordinate amount of time pondering and writing out the assigned punishment.

When we do decide to punish, one consequence for bad behavior is for the offender to do the victim's bidding three times that day. In other words, the offender may be asked by the victim to do one of his or her chores, or scratch his or her back, or serve him or her in some way. What a great way to develop humility! This can be entertaining for the parents to observe as well.

When there is a disturbance between children and passions are raging, I often find it good to channel those passions by separating the children and giving them some brief physical exercises to do. By expending energy and attention in the physical exercise, their anger and irritability quickly wanes.

We never use prayer or scripture reading as a form of punishment as we do not wish to associate the things of God with negative connotations.

Generally, whenever I find children arguing over a material possession, I will immediately confiscate and often discard that possession. I do not want my children to be materialists and will not stand for them fighting over things. Even if the material possession has a significant value and purpose, I will still not hesitate to discard it as the lesson, as well as the persons involved, are much more important than the thing.

On the topic of materialism, since our reversion we have never allowed shopping to be perceived as a source of entertainment or relaxation for our children. When it is necessary to shop we try to get what we need and move on as quickly as possible. We are trying to form our children not to be materialists. We happily utilize the gifts God has given us that we need to live, but try to see everything as a means to live God's will as opposed to an end in themselves. Our hearts are reserved for God. "For where your treasure is, there will your hearts be also." (Luke 12:34)

With regard to formation of our older children, they essentially only need some prayer, guidance, reminders, and encouragement to live virtue, as they have already received a solid foundation, and have made their faith and formation their own. They exercise their freedom and growing maturity to challenge themselves to live God's will. Although it is never too late to form children at any age, it is certainly *much easier to start at infancy*. Depending on the situation, there can and still needs to be a certain degree of imposition where necessary to guide and protect our adolescents and teenagers, yet they ideally need to buy into their own formation and good, objectively true values. It is also important for teenagers as well as the youngest children to witness their parents' *uncompromising witness* in living according to the *hierarchy of values* they have taught and inculcated in their family. Leadership and the testimony of one's life in this regard are crucial.

Usually whenever we buy candy or ice cream, we will select one, two, or three of the children whose behavior or accomplishments have been exemplary in some way, and we will award that treat to that select individual or individuals as opposed to the entire family. We will then announce that it is up to the prizewinners to decide if they will share their prize with the other children. I really do not think I can recall even one time where the child did not share, and they typically share equally, at least relatively so, not keeping more (or much more) for themselves than for the others.

Therefore, we try to use a positive pedagogy to instill and build good moral habits. Obviously, here you have the motivation to be good and to excel at endeavors, which will often result in achieving a reward, while at the same time the children are learning to share selflessly.

I like to give the children nicknames and have come to use this means as a form of encouragement to live a virtue, or sometimes simply as a term of endearment, and sometimes simply representative of the child's personality. Admittedly the nicknames became more virtuous after I had my reversion to the faith, so the older children's aren't profound, but denote affection in their own way. Some of the nicknames we have used are *Shanner* for Shannon, *Scarlet* for Tara, *Gracer* for Grace, *Leener* for Colleen, *Deir the Dear*, *Munchkin,* or *Little Bird* for Deirdre, Bridget *the Great*, Shane *the Strong* or *Shaney-Boy*, *Diligent Fiona* or *Holy*, Maura *the Magnificent* or *Fighting Irish*, *Smiley* Clare or Clare *the Conqueror*, Patrick *the Powerful, Sweetie* or *the Beautiful One for* Mairead, *Wildcat* for Brighde, and *Gentle One* for Shealagh.

I encourage the children not to be tattle-tellers. For example, when someone would tattle on my daughter Colleen, I began the tradition of a statement that goes something like, "I will never believe anything bad about Colleen." It was amusing to watch little Colleen sit there amazed, perhaps guilty as charged, but seeing her father's confidence in her. I believe that this is an encouragement for the child to live better the virtue her father sees in her.

I have also encouraged my children by telling them they are leaders. They have often reacted in a disbelieving manner, but I found that the more I told them that they were leaders, the more this talent would emerge, and of course I meant it; they are leaders.

We have used various points and rewards systems. We change the system often as we find that these programs will get stale after time and need to be reinvented. They do work well.

For example we have had considerable success daily using competition as a motivator. It is often boys versus girls with our younger children. When I wake them up in the morning, I will announce that there will be one point each for whatever team gets out of bed and on their feet first, either boys or girls. (Usually, the boys win, simply because they are extremely competitive.) When a certain point level is achieved there will be a reward, usually a surprise of some sort. Surprises work best in case some of the children are not particularly intrigued by the preannounced prize. The

FORMATION OF CHILDREN

mystery increases the attractiveness of the prize as well.

Next we will have a contest for which team will be ready and down for breakfast first. Before coming down for breakfast, the team's room must be completely organized and cleaned up with beds made. The children must be fully dressed, faces washed, teeth brushed, and hair nicely combed. I often remind them that if they accomplish all their morning responsibilities early with a little time to spare, we will have a football or running bases game before Mass once we get to the church. This is a great motivator. This all creates great family unity and joy with everyone coming together to play a game, which happens almost on a daily basis.

In our family, everyone plays together, from one-year-olds up to adults. For example, we will be throwing the football around and little Brighde, age one, will come up excited and yelling "ball," and we will put the big football in her baby hands and watch the delight on her face as she *throws* it by dropping it on the ground and running after it as it rolls. *It is a great joy every time a new child is born into a family*. The family can never again imagine itself without that child as an integral part.

Before leaving for Mass in the mornings, be it a school day or not, the house must be straightened and all the kitchen jobs done. Everyone has their particular responsibility. We have a *family manual* with periodically updated time schedules and tasks. This *family manual* first came into existence when Kathleen was on bed rest with the twins in 1997, and is referred to in detail in the *How We Came to be a Family Chapter*. Frankly, out of selfishness and survival, I decided that there was no way I was going to do all the chores around the house myself, so I very quickly discovered that the *children were capable of much more than we had given them credit for* up until that time. I am convinced that giving children challenging and demanding responsibilities brings many positive benefits for that child, not to mention the family. The child grows in generosity, maturity, and the capacity for sacrifice. In short, he or she begins to acquire the capacity for greatness. *Nothing worthwhile is accomplished without sacrifice.*

In terms of intellectual formation, we encourage our children that to do their best in school is their God-given duty. For the most part, our children have received excellent grades with very little help from or reliance on their parents. I think that because of the work and responsibility the children take on from an early age in our household, they develop a concrete maturity and commitment to do their best, as well as skills and virtues such as organization, responsibility, diligence, and time management. Some of our children struggle a bit more than the others in this regard, but this is all part of the diverse dynamics of the family in accordance with God's beautiful plan.

We give our children opportunities to use their minds and imaginations and enjoy the great outdoors. We encourage them to read good books. They are avid readers. We take out thirty to forty library books at a time, all needing the moral approval of a well-formed, reliable family member, such as an older child or parent. Our children at times spontaneously create and perform plays for our family as well as for neighboring families or guests.

We also work on the human formation of our children, which includes such things as manners, physical appearance, and dignity. We try to have them dress for the occasion, always with a neat, clean, chaste, and virtuous appearance. Human formation is important as it speaks to the *dignity of the human person*, both our own dignity and the dignity of others. Our physical appearance and manners proclaim the respect we have for ourselves and others. This is very much a lost art today. This is a work in progress for the Littleton family, but at least we have the road map to the destination.

We work at manners at the table and like to have fun with it by jokingly competing and catching each other in infractions such as having an elbow on the table, failing to have a napkin on the lap, or speaking with food in one's mouth. There is to be no *slurping, burping, or chirping at the table*. Intelligent and soft-spoken conversation is encouraged, but no earsplitting, piercing noise. There is no getting up from the table until one is excused.

Of course we pray grace before and after meals. The praying of grace in public settings as well as at home is quite natural. We have been doing this for so many years that concern for human respect is no longer an issue. Somehow the devil is able to fool many good people with the lie that somehow they should be embarrassed or uncomfortable with praying in public; that they should always hide their faith, and keep it to themselves. This falsehood is something I certainly experienced when we first began to pray grace in public. In actuality, however, why should we feel the least bit uneasy about doing something as natural and simple as praying to God, Our Father, giving him thanks for his many gifts? He deserves this, and he is in command, so we should have no worries about what "they" might think. *Just who are the infamous "they' anyway?* I don't think "they" will be there with their lawyers to defend us relative to all the decisions we made in our lives in acquiescence to the mysterious morally relativistic will of "they" when, upon our deaths, we are judged. Where will "they" be then?

We train our children in critical thinking, often engaging them in conversations on this subject. This is vitally important. For example, we will bring up a current event or something we came across in the media, and then examine it with a critical eye for the truth, for how it measures up to God's supernatural view. We will examine perhaps what the agenda of the writer might have been. We will talk about the influences perhaps of the dominant culture, or a morally relativistic cultural view that is being expressed, and how it compares with the objective truth. We will look at how the event, article, or movie measures up to our

Christian morality. This is a superb exercise in helping the children develop critical thinking and discernment skills that they will need throughout their lives. They will eventually need to stand on their own two feet to discern the truth and live by it.

We try to always make decisions in our family based on our Christian faith. This often entails sacrifice. For example one of the children might suggest we go to a particular store to go shopping for something when another family member will point out that it is Sunday and we do not do unnecessary shopping on the Lord's Day. Or a new movie may have come out that their friends have talked about seeing, and we as parents will point out that based on our research there is something inappropriate for children in that movie, and that therefore they will not be permitted to see it. These are small sacrifices, but these lessons are building a foundation for the children to form them to be willing and able to *stand up for their faith, for their beliefs, even when it is costly to do so.*

I have often admired the martyrs throughout history who have courageously given their lives for the truth, for their faith, sometimes enduring indescribable tortures, but not giving in unto death. Certainly these martyrs needed a tremendous grace from God to be able to persevere and lay down their lives. I believe, however, that *these heroic martyrdoms were merely the culmination of many years of forming their wills through sacrifices in little day-to-day things.* I do not believe anyone gets to the point of great, heroic sacrifice if he was not formed over time in sacrifice in the *little things*, formed in the school of putting God's will first in every decision and act, even in the seemingly *little things*. "Well done good and faithful servant: you have shown you can be faithful in small things, I will trust you with greater; come and join in your master's happiness." (Matthew 25:21)

In our family we have a system of formation we call *charges and charge-masters. Charge-masters* are older children who bear responsibility for a younger child or infant. They are expected to help to form that *charge* in virtue. They are also expected to serve them in various ways such as assisting with getting them ready and dressed in the morning, getting their shoes on, getting them into the van, supervising them, getting them ready for bed at night, seeing that their faces are washed, teeth brushed, etc. This is of great benefit to the family in that the work is distributed in such a way as to not overwhelm the individual *charge-master* or the parents. The *charge-master* helps to share the load with the parent. Obviously the *charges* benefit from the help and formation they are offered. The *charge-masters* grow in responsibility, charity and a spirit of sacrifice and service. This is a great means of overcoming self-centeredness and selfishness. This also creates *imperishable bonds* between the children. It is almost like the children are blessed with additional parents.

We truly believe that this is the way that God designed a family to function. We are aware that some people think we are demanding too much and overburdening our children, that we should let them be kids, let them do what they want and enjoy themselves. We strongly disagree with these negative assessments, and are convinced that *we are doing a great service to our children by giving them these responsibilities*. In fact, Kathleen and I do not know how a family could be run without giving older children responsibilities, and we are confident that any large family would support and attest to our philosophy based on their own experience.

FORMATION OF CHILDREN

We have truly been blessed with the gift of a large family, and with this blessing comes a great responsibility, to raise them in the way they should go. As parents, God has given each of us not only the responsibility, but also the graces, to be the primary formators of our children. "Parents are the first and most important educators of their children, and they also possess a fundamental competency in this area: they are educators because they are parents." (*The Truth and Meaning of Human Sexuality #23*, Pontifical Council for the Family) We cannot completely delegate this to anyone, not to a caregiver, grandparent, babysitter, or teacher. As Catholic parents we are trying to raise our children to be leaders for the world and the Church in today's society. Our family needs to live in the world, but not be of the world. We need to take the narrow path that leads to life, eternal life, even when, and especially when it means not doing what every one else is doing; even if this means being *radically different*.

We have a *duty to protect our children*. We need to realize and live up to the fact that we as parents have the *right and duty* to decide what is appropriate for our children and what is not. For example, under the principle of *subsidiarity,* no school authority has the right to require that our children or anyone's children be involved in something we as parents do not believe is appropriate, such as for example an explicit sex-ed program. "Subsidiarity thus complements paternal and maternal love and confirms its fundamental nature, inasmuch as all other participants in the process of education are only able to carry out their responsibilities *in the name of the parents, with their consent* and, to a certain degree, *with their authorization"* (*The Truth and Meaning of Human Sexuality #23*, Pontifical Council for the Family)

We believe that for the most part, sex education programs in schools are inappropriate; in other words that the setting of the school to form children in sex-education is the improper venue. Kathleen and I would personally make an exception for a dignified, non-graphic, age-appropriate true chastity program for adolescents or teens, such as based on Servant of God, John Paul II's Theology of the Body, with the appropriate teacher or formator and environment.

As a general rule, we believe that the subject of sex-education is most appropriately handled in the home by the parents, one-on-one with the child, at the time and

Formation of Children

to the degree the child is ready. Every child is at a different, unique level of innocence and stage of development. Furthermore many sex-education programs present values very much in conflict with the beliefs of the parents. Even a relatively innocuous sex-ed program at a school has the intrinsic problem that it is being administered in a group setting. The material and discussion will almost certainly be presented at a level that is not appropriate for the level of development and state of soul of individual children in the class. The group setting will generally lead to questions being presented by certain children who have a greater sexual knowledge and perhaps even experience than others in the class, and this becomes a source of degradation of the innocence and dignity of those more innocent children. Once certain ideas and images are impressed upon the mind and memory, there is no going back, and these can become an occasion of sin, and of acting out. Innocence is a fragile gift, and we have an obligation to protect this in our children *who rely on us*.

Rather than retreating from the world, we want our children to be apostles in changing the culture and their peers for the better, and they have worked hard at this.

We have engaged them in many opportunities in this regard in their schools, clubs, and service projects. However when an environment such as at a particular school or class is irreparably immoral we have the right, and in our estimation, the responsibility to opt our children out of any program that we, as parents, deem inappropriate; and if necessary to go to the extent even to opt them out of the particular school, perhaps changing schools where that is a viable option, or perhaps even to homeschool where possible. With regard to school environment, we believe that as parents we should do everything we can to change things for the better, but when reasonable or even extraordinary efforts are made by both parents and children, and little, no, or insufficient positive change is experienced then it is time to look at the other options above. Our duty is to *try* to improve the environment and culture in the venues and circumstances we are involved in, but this does not mean that in every case we will be successful. "Whatever town or village you go into ask for someone trustworthy and stay with him until you leave. As you enter his house, salute it, and if the house deserves it, let your peace descend upon it; if it does not, let your peace come back to you. And if anyone does not welcome you, or listen to what you have to say, as you walk out of the house or town shake the dust from your feet." (Matthew 10:11-16)

Our first duty is to the protection and well-being of the children God has entrusted to us. In situations where an extreme immoral environment exists it is an error to think that our child's presence alone, even if he or she is the most well-formed and zealous leader, will be enough to measurably change the system for the better. In such a dissolute atmosphere it is unfortunately usually the child that is changed. We believe that the cost of one's innocence and perhaps the cost of one's very faith and soul is a price too high to pay.

Reflect on the "boiled frog" syndrome. When a frog is to be cooked, expert chefs know that if you simply drop the live frog in a pot of boiling water, the frog will jump right out. But by putting the frog in lukewarm water first, and then slowly raising the heat over a period of time, the frog docilely stays in the environment, not recognizing the inevitable end ... a dead boiled frog, ready to be devoured. By keeping one's child in an extreme environment that constantly day in and day out exposes him or her to poor peer groups that revel in profanity, promiscuity, impurity of dress, poor attitude, and lack of motivation, as well as to teachers that may themselves have and live entirely different values than the parents, and are ingraining the students with their own principles such as moral relativism, is one truly living up to one's God-given responsibility as a parent?

We are not saying that at the first sign of any problem a parent should opt his child out of a class or a school. The perfect educational and cultural environment does not exist, but nonetheless, a parent has to use their *best judgment along with much prayer* to discern whether they are being called to a more drastic intervention in their child's formation and education, and if so, be willing to act in the best interests of their child, even when unpopular, significant measures are necessary.

Our children are our treasure, our pearls. I am not calling anyone a name here, but I believe this may be one of the lessons Christ meant to convey when he said, "Do not throw your pearls in front of pigs, or they may trample them and then turn on you and tear you to pieces." (Matthew 7:6) When we permit our children to be degraded in a detrimental environment, be it in school or with peer groups, their innocence, dignity, and very personhood is being trampled. And the result is an increasingly relativistic, and immoral dominant culture that is hostile and ready to tear to pieces the very concept that objective moral truth exists. The institution of the family itself also becomes ever more an anathema. *If enough parents are increasingly able and willing to discern and act in defense of what they know to be best for their children, to stand up for the rights of their family, the culture will begin to gradually respond and change for the better.*

As parents we should take reasonable efforts to educate ourselves. We are not required, however, to research, prove, and intellectually win over or convert school authorities and the so-called experts with regard to a program we do not want our children exposed to. Our gut feelings are good enough. Why? Because God has given us this authority as parents, and he has also given us the graces such that even our instincts alone are usually sufficient. And this of course does not apply only to school settings, but rather to every aspect of our children's lives.

As parents, Kathleen and I refuse to compromise the good of our children when it comes to their protection. Our children depend on us, on *our judgment*. We cannot allow ourselves to be unduly influenced by the purported experts to compromise on our moral beliefs. This calls for parents, with God's help, to be courageous, to be willing to go against the current of popular opinion, to do what is right to protect our children, not only their physical well-being, but even more importantly, their innocence and very souls. Candidly, although we would prefer not to be forced to make such a choice, Kathleen and I would, if necessary, prefer to have academically under-educated children with solid moral and spiritual formation than have children with a first-class academic education, but morally and spiritually degraded.

It is through prayer, and for Catholics the sacraments, especially the Eucharist, that God opens our eyes to these truths and gives us the fortitude and courage to live up to our duty.

An example of another area from our own experience would be relatives or friends at a party having an inappropriate conversation, or watching something on television that we believe is inappropriate for our family. We have had to make quickly enforced decisions to remove our children from the presence of the conversation or the television or to leave the party altogether when necessary. Some would argue that children are going to be exposed to certain evils no matter what we do, so why worry about it. It is true that they will be exposed to some evils. Even driving down the road, one encounters very inappropriate and impure billboards. We teach our children to control their eyes, thoughts, and imaginations, but undoubtedly they will catch a glimpse from time to time quite accidentally. Nonetheless, Kathleen and I believe it is incumbent upon us to do everything we can to protect the innocence of our children to the extent we can. I believe someone said that the average person will consume a pound of dirt before they die. While this may be true, this does not mean that we should intentionally serve up a meal of dirt or sprinkle dirt as a condiment on our food. *We avoid eating dirt and we should avoid those things that internally harm the innocence and malform the consciences of our children.*

In 1996, we decided to do away with commercial television in our home, and it has been totally freeing In other words, we have a television, but no cable or antenna. I still remember calling the cable company to cancel our service, and the customer service person having a very difficult time comprehending that I truly wanted to cancel cable altogether. He kept trying to figure out which premium choice channels I wanted cancelled, and it took him some time to finally understand that I wanted to cancel cable altogether.

I don't think I have to convince anyone of the anti-Christian, immoral values that are powerfully presented through many programs on television. I am convinced that there is a great desensitizing of the masses, but in spite of this I think many people would still agree that there are many inappropriate programs on television. To borrow someone else's analogy, would you ever invite a guest on a daily basis into the house who constantly barraged your family with undignified, immoral, and impure comments and examples? Yet there is the television, with many programs pouring poison into the hearts and minds of our family, and our most innocent little ones. And we are fooling ourselves if we think that any of us adults are so smart and strong that we are above being influenced and changed ourselves by constant exposure to these things.

We are not saying that all television is bad. Television is not intrinsically evil, but it needs to be put to its proper use for the good. There are many beautiful, educational, dignified, quality secular and religious programs that can be quite edifying. For those families that can control television in its current state and take only what is good, using it in moderation, my hat is off to you. We were not able to do this.

I am also aware that a significant motivator in holding onto commercial television even in those families who have seriously considered doing away with it is the powerful cultural pull of sports for men. I theorize that many men love watching sports so much, in part because they are consoled by and have nostalgia for good experiences they had in their childhood in a more innocent era, perhaps with their fathers, in watching and talking about sports. A reality check along these lines, however, might be to seriously ask what our fathers some decades ago (before perhaps they themselves became desensitized) would have done if we their children would have been exposed to some of the graphic sexual and undignified commercials that are prevalent during sports programs today. *We as fathers have a grave duty to protect our children*, and sometimes the action called for is *costly*. What father would not hurl himself into grave risk to protect his child if he or she was being physically attacked? *Yet, I maintain that the attacks against the purity, chastity, innocence, and spiritual sensitivity of our children are worse and of greater consequence than any physical attack*. We cannot settle for what the media is pouring into our households today. It is time for a drastic response to a serious matter. If enough people were willing to turn off, disconnect, tune out, or get rid of television we would have an impetus for change for the better.

Certainly work can, should, and is being done to bring good morals back into television and the media in general. I am not asserting that society should do away with this technology. But in its current condition the Littleton family places a higher value on protecting our children than on having the use of commercial and cable television. Doing away with commercial and cable television has actually not been difficult whatsoever for us. We really never missed it.

Some will argue that we are out of touch with the news and current events by not having television. This is not true in that we get all of the news we need via the newspaper, radio, and internet, although these must be closely and carefully monitored as well. There is a great trend today to be news-mongers, where one's curiosity is never sufficiently satiated. We believe that even the news should be consumed in vigilant moderation.

I have no idea how we would fit television back into our lives. Having been away from it so long, when I am exposed to television at a public place, I have a strong sensitivity to the powerful pull and hypnotizing effect of television. Even if we had been able to control it to the extent that nothing inappropriate would ever be viewed by any member of our family, I would still not want commercial television in our home because I know it would pull us into spending inordinate amounts of time watching it. Time is precious collateral that we bear a grave responsibility for before God when we are judged.

We need eyes to see these things, to live by a proper hierarchy of values, and I am convinced this only comes through God's grace. That is why we must be people of prayer and for those of us who are Catholics, men and women of the sacraments, especially the sacraments of Reconciliation and the Eucharist.

We have a VCR and more recently a DVD player on which to play wholesome movies. One of our favorite unifying activities as a family is to have a movie night. We have found that over the years, even our teenagers' lives have stayed centered around the family, and that we enjoy doing things like this together. We have developed a DVD and VHS library of classic movies. We have also discovered a significant number of modern movies that are full of virtue, and very inspiring to watch. We are quite selective and find unfortunately that most movies being produced today are not appropriate for our family, although some are very good.

We do have a love for good movies in our family, and this has been an influence on our eldest daughter's interest in pursuing a degree in media at a Catholic university on the west coast. Our eldest daughter and the founders of the university she is attending recognize the power of the media to influence the culture, and the need for talented, educated persons with strong Christian morals working within the industry in order to better it.

We also control the internet. We eventually got our cable service back in order to have high-speed internet access, but without hooking up our television. Besides using certain filters, we have strictly controlled our children's access to the internet all the way through the end of high school. Our children are good children, and we trust them, however we also understand that it is

FORMATION OF CHILDREN

not only possible but very easy to stumble upon inappropriate and impure images and websites quite by accident. Additionally we understand human nature and the powerful draw and temptation of sexual material. As the Church teaches us, we must do what is in our power to avoid occasions of sin. Therefore, none of our children through high school have had access to the internet without a parent being with them to get them on the site they need to fulfill a homework assignment.

Our computers are in public areas of the house. These are indeed extreme measures; however, there is a lot at stake. Our children have not missed out as they are all computer literate in line with their particular age, but none are addicted to the computer or internet.

We do not allow any video games whatsoever, nor use of I-pods in our family. We never have, and we have never missed them.

We do enjoy in moderation dignified, wholesome, and beautiful music. Our family members of all ages seem to have the same taste. The children also enjoy singing together in the car, often with even the older ones joining in or leading.

As a family we do not believe in retreating into a *fortress mentality*, but rather to engage the world and transform it for Christ. As Christians and others of strong and Godly moral values, we are not to be on the defensive. We are not to be afraid. Jesus Christ said to Peter that the gates of hell can never hold out against his Church. (Cf: Matthew 16:18) As a priest once said to us, what enemy has ever attacked using gates as an effective offensive weapon? No, the devil, the enemy, the agitator, the divider, and liar is afraid, and on the defensive. We need to know this and be confident and courageous in standing up for what we know to be right.

However, we do believe that we need to fortify our children with the necessary formation, faith, dignity, and confidence before we send then out to transform the world. Otherwise the world may transform (malform) them. As someone has said, one completes the building of a ship before sending it out onto rough seas.

I wish to address another issue. Even good things, engaged in to a disordered degree, can have adverse effects. We are convinced that a mind exposed to constant stimulation of noise, music, television, video games, I-pods, etc. becomes *desensitized*. *This desensitization of mind and spirit has a grave adverse effect on the interior life, and even on one's ability to think and reflect.* This certainly harms one's ability to pray, to have an interior conversation and experience with God. Our children love to read books, play outdoors, play board games, create plays, in short, to use their minds and imaginations over being fed by a technological source of mental entertainment. They have a beautiful spiritual capacity as well. Kathleen and I love to pray, read, and experience nature. I like to go for runs, exercise, and play sports with the children.

In our family we try to transmit the reality of the dignity of the human person made in God's image, where purity and chastity is understood more in a positive sense than in the "thou shall nots." We are made in the image and likeness of God. We are temples of the Holy Spirit. Our sexuality is a beautiful gift, but reserved for its ordered use. "...Modesty exists as an intuition of the supernatural dignity proper to man. It is born in the awakening consciousness of being a subject. Teaching modesty to children and adolescents means awakening in them respect for the human person." (CCC 2524)

In our family, modest clothing is a must. Our bodies are temples of the Holy Spirit. Kathleen and I must approve of everything our children wear. By the grace of God, I am never hesitant about challenging clothing that I deem inappropriate. We set our standards high and will challenge the little things so that the significant things will not even make it to the radar screen. Having said this, our children dress stylishly, not prudishly, but with dignity.

I also, albeit not often enough, look for opportunities to complement the beauty of my daughters, and to tell our sons that they are handsome. I will also go out of my way to genuinely complement a particularly beautiful, but ladylike outfit that one of my daughter's may be wearing as a means of positive motivation. Our daughters need to hear this. If they never hear this from their fathers they might be more lured to go looking for attention in the wrong ways and places.

We have made an effort to form our children in chastity and modesty from the earliest age in the way they dress and in what they are exposed to. We also form them by giving them opportunities to stand up for their faith in this regard. For example, in most grocery stores today there are magazines displayed at the check out lines, many of which have covers with inappropriate, immodest images of women as well as men. We do what we can to avoid having the children exposed to these images by moving them quickly past the magazines, engaging them in the work of unloading the cart, and having them step through to the end of the conveyor belt. Interestingly, the magazines are positioned at eye level of children.

As their father, I have on many occasions invited my children, on their own at as young as age seven, to find the store manager to encourage the removal of the inappropriate magazines from the checkout lines. The scenario usually goes something like this. My children in a band of two or three will approach the main desk. I will watch from a close proximity, allowing them do this on their own so that they will build courage and confidence in standing up for their beliefs. The employee behind the desk will usually initially ignore the children or not notice them. Eventually they get the employee's attention. The employee will look a little surprised and perhaps patronizingly listen to them. The children will express that they would like to talk with the manager about the impure magazines at the checkout counter. At this point the employee will begin to look more serious and will summon the manager, or it may become necessary for me to step in and charitably encourage him or her to do so.

When the manager arrives, the children, usually on their own, and sometimes with my assistance, will express that it is not right to have impure magazines at the checkout counter and that they should be moved. The manager will listen politely and invite the children or myself to fill out a form for the corporate office. Sometimes the manager will indicate that he will look into the possibility of having the magazines moved.

I'm not sure if our efforts have ever succeeded in having the magazines moved, however, I do not believe that this should dissuade us in our efforts. Personally I believe, as I mentioned, that my children are gaining by this experience. Secondly, I believe we should all do what we can to stand up for what is right. *We do not have an obligation to be successful, but only to do what is within our power. We leave the results to God.* Sometimes we are merely planting a seed that will have its effect later on. Obviously, if enough men, women, and children of good will were to lodge similar complaints we would see the magazines swiftly removed. This methodology could be applied to innumerable situations in society.

It is a tradition in our family that our children do not date until they are at least eighteen. Once they are eighteen, they really do not date either. In our family, we *court*. We feel that the current cultural phenomenon of dating is, in our opinion, highly problematic. It is seen as a form of entertainment and socializing. The idea seems to be to get to know the opposite sex by dating numerous individuals. This is often happening during the junior high and high school years when there is no realistic possibility of marriage.

The difference with *courting* is that it occurs when the individuals are of an age to discern a spouse and follow through with marriage. Otherwise, when you have two young people, alone and unsupervised with hormones and passions raging, you have what we would identify as an occasion of sin. In other words, you are playing with fire. We have to know ourselves and our weaknesses. To place even a virtuous young person repeatedly in a situation like this along with all the peer pressure involved, one has to admit that there is a noteworthy risk of falling into premarital sexual activity, as happens so frequently in the dominant culture today.

We are convinced that it is much better to court, as we believe was the tradition in most cultures for many centuries. We define *courting* not as casual dating, but rather a time in which a young man and woman of age to discern a spouse, and suspecting that the other might be the spouse God intended for him or her from all eternity, spend time together in a group setting. If the young person is living at home, this is best done in the presence of the family for the most part. If the young person is away at school or working, this is best done in a group of young people. Certainly the couple can break off for private conversation to get to know each other better, but preferably not where they would be alone for an extended period of time.

We even strongly believe that kissing on the lips should be reserved for marriage. What a beautiful kiss it would be if the kiss exchanged in the marriage ceremony would be the first kiss. Well yes, we will permit and even encourage the man to chastely kiss his beloved's hand once they are engaged. Yes, I am absolutely serious!

We encourage our children, if they are called to marriage, to pray that God will arrange for them to find a spouse with a strong faith, maturity, and a capacity to sacrifice. These qualities seem to be rare today, but the magnificent capacity for these virtues exists in every person. We each need to do what we can to improve the culture. *Humanity needs to rediscover its dignity and potential, and this will only begin with prayer.*

We seem to have had some success in forming a *family culture* where the *family is at the center*. Our children have not gotten involved in the teen party scene. They do socialize, but with friends of their own sex in a supervised setting. For example, they are members of Catholic boys and girls clubs where the children and parents have similar values to ours. These clubs offer programs for the young people to be apostolically active by getting out into the communities to help people in service projects, such as assisting the elderly in nursing homes, doing door-to-door evangelizing missions, and working with youth in economically depressed areas. Our children are not in the least socially deprived. As a matter of fact, their maturity level, by the grace of God, is astounding. *The dominant culture today tends to vastly underestimate the capacity of youth.* It assumes that youth will be lazy, self-centered, immature, disrespectful, etc. This does not have to be, and this is not the way God has made them.

The choice of college is critical in our family. We have encouraged our children to attend universities that teach and maintain a culture of high Christian values, and in our case, the unadulterated Catholic faith. At the Catholic university that some of our children have attended, they offer a beautiful and dignified nineteenth-century ball. The young ladies and gentlemen come together in a group dressed in a chaste and distinguished manner, and have a wonderful evening with stately dancing and an opportunity to get to know each other. The young people love this.

The dominant culture on campuses such as these tends to be for the most part, morally upright as opposed to the party and illicit sex and drinking scene on so many campuses. How many good young people have lost their faith and morals during their college experience? Again, we are human, and to immerse a virtuous young person into a dominant culture that is morally corrupt comes with an incredible risk of a gradual degradation of the young person's morals. Yes, our young people are going to have to live in the world, but I repeat, let's finish building the ship before sending it out into rough seas.

On another subject, we do not get involved in a lot of extracurricular activities such as organized team sports in our family life. When these are engaged in to a disordered degree, they do tremendous damage to family unity. *The soccer or baseball coach is not The Way, The Truth, and The Life. Baseball or dance is not the living bread that came down from heaven. Jesus Christ did not say that whoever excels in a variety of sports will be raised on the last day.* We are not claiming that these things are not good and healthy in *moderation*, but that we need to examine our priorities and strike a *balance*. God has given us a fixed number of hours in each day, and we need to prioritize our time and make some *radical sacrifices for a greater good*. When families are running at such a pace that they seldom have time to be together as a complete family, sit down to meals together, pray together, and recreate as a complete family unit, there is something askew.

God and family come first, in that order. Why should we let our children and their activities run the family around by the nose to physical, mental, emotional, and spiritual exhaustion? There is nothing we can give to our children to make up for the time we should be spending with them. *They need us, not things, and they need each other as well.*

We form our children in charity. Unfortunately I often fall short in example as their father in this area with my ongoing struggles with impatience and a very passionate temperament. Nonetheless, we are always *working and insisting on charity* in our household, from ourselves and from the children themselves, as well as the trait that is indispensable for the good and unity of any family – *speedy forgiveness*. Albeit not perfectly, we exercise the virtue of saying we are sorry and forgiving swiftly. We raise our children to think and speak well of each other and of others outside the family; and to always think the best of others, presuming the best, exercising compassion and mercy. We strive to hate the sin, but to always, always, love the sinner. We all require mercy and forgiveness from God and we must therefore be wiling to give it.

An example of an incident of selflessness and charity in our family was when our three-year-old vomited in the middle of the night. I heard some commotion, got up and found that my sixteen-year-old and fourteen-year-old daughters were cleaning up and giving my son a bath without intending to wake Kathleen and me.

FORMATION OF CHILDREN

When our twin daughters, Maura and Clare, were five-years-old one of them won an award on the last day of school. When the other twin was asked how she felt about her twin sister winning the award, she responded with a big smile, "I was just so happy for her!"

Although there can be and are fights and arguments in our family, as there can be in any family, our children are truly each other's best friends.

We have just offered various *practical* beliefs, ideas, and methodologies, but *we have a grave duty to tell you that these will not get anyone very far without an essential ingredient; that is God's grace and help.* Where do we get that? Through prayer, and again, for those of us who are Catholic, especially through the source and summit of the Christian life - the Eucharist – the Body, Blood, Soul, and Divinity of Jesus Christ.

We must build our lives and the formation of our families on a strong prayer and sacramental life. The justifications for not following through with this must be thrown down and trampled in the dirt with our heels. "The flesh is weak" indeed, as Christ said, so let's not fool ourselves. We need to be awake, out of the fog of our excuses and the misleading dominant culture, and come to reality. We need to pray. As busy as we are, we must pray, as Christ did throughout his busy life, even as he prayed the psalms in the process of dying in the midst of immense pain. "Into your hands I commit my spirit." (Psalm 31:5) "My God, my God, why have you deserted me?" (Psalm 22:1) (Both of these psalms in full context are prayers of *hope and trust* in God.) *He turned his pain into Love through prayer.* If we do not pray and take advantage of the sacraments we will remain the weaklings that we are. But if we do, we will receive the supernatural strength that we need, from Christ, the source of everything. Have hope. We must have hope. *This world is dying of starvation for hope.*

Like in the movie *Spiderman II*, we need to come out of the fog and regain our sight. Perhaps you have seen the movie; Spiderman fell into self-denial of his supernatural vocation, into mediocrity. He ended up in a fog. *He had to put his human eyeglasses on, because he had lost his supernatural vision.*

When we don't pray, we lose focus, we lose touch with the supernatural help we have available to live our vocation and talents to the ultimate. When we don't pray we lose our vital connection. Like Spiderman, our powers are lost, and when we try to jump to the next high-rise building, we are powerless and we fall sixty stories and slam onto the pavement below. Our *supernatural capacity* is gone because *we made excuses and tried to tame our vocation in life* and retreated to the deception of a life of comfort, ignoring those who *depend on us to lead, be strong, and protect them*. Others, especially our families, depend on us for their very lives. Will we trade our vocation, our potential, our fullness of life, and our very children for a comfortable and pleasure-filled life? What will we have left to give them? We will be empty!

We need to have Jesus Christ shining through us to give light to our families and to others. We must give our family, neighbors, coworkers, and the culture at large something that counts. When we pray and make use of the sacraments, when we lead Eucharistic lives, when we feed on Christ, we become more giving, more apostolic, more serving. We may be punched around by a huge eight-armed villain as was Spiderman, but *we won't give in*. Like Spiderman, when he began again to live his *supernatural vocation*, we are *invincible*. We must not give in. We need to fight and win with the help of Jesus Christ. *There is too much at stake!*

Listen, we are unbeatable with God. In addition to "Do not be afraid," what other word in common did the angels say to Zechariah, the Blessed Virgin Mary, and the shepherds in the *Gospel of St. Luke*? "*Listen.*" In other words, pray, have faith, listen to God, put on your *supernatural outlook* so God can act and do something big, something transcendent, with you, with your life! To listen we must learn to cultivate silence both externally and internally. We have to step out of our habits, make regular time to be alone and with our family to pray, turn off the noise, the radio, television, computer, ad nauseam frivolous conversations, and learn to invite the Holy Spirit as the sweet guest into our minds and hearts to help us push out the internal racket of a thousand scattered distractions, thoughts, and worries.

We must create an environment that permits the Holy Spirit to *rest* in us. God is a God of peace. *He wants to find rest in us so he can transform us.* He *rests* in us and we *rest* in him. He is then able to give us true *peace*. We then learn to be in constant company with him, and docile to what he wants to do with us, like Simeon, "The Holy Spirit *rested (emphasis added)* on him. It had been revealed to him by the Holy Spirit that he would not see death until he had set his eyes on the Christ of the Lord. Prompted by the Spirit he came to the Temple: and when the parents brought in the child Jesus to do for him what the law required, he took him into his arms and blessed God; and he said: 'Now, Master you can let your servant go in peace.'" (Luke 2:25-29)

Simeon had cultivated in his life an environment where the Holy Spirit could find *rest* in his soul and transform him into the *masterpiece God had intended from all eternity*. He therefore became so detached, so transformed, so much in union with Christ, so sanctified, happy, and at peace that from the depths of his soul he proclaimed that he was so totally fulfilled he was ready for death at any moment God called him. He was *invincible, and feared nothing because he had Everything; he had God himself.*

Don't be afraid. With Christ even death is defeated. The more transformed we are into Christ, the more our will is merged with his, as Christ's will was merged with the Father's will: "let your will be done not mine," (Luke 22:43) as Jesus said in the garden of Gethsemane. God our Father is with us. He even goes to the *extreme in his love* by sending *angels* to assist us as he did with Christ in his agony. If we will only *listen* and allow God to act, we will have the *supernatural outlook* to know and count on this help that is always present, "Then an angel appeared to him, coming from heaven to give him strength." (Luke 22:44)

Saint Paul, patron of apostles and Christians, had this *supernatural connection*. He did not rely on his own power. He was *radically dependent on God*. He boasted in his weakness. He said that he was a "nobody." (2 Corinthians 12) Yet Saint Paul proclaimed, "There is nothing I cannot master with the help of the One who gives me strength." (Philippians 4:13) *Prayer and the sacraments are the fuel of our being.* We need them to fuel and fortify our will for our God-ordained mission.

Whatever is good in the Littleton family is by the grace of God. *Whatever is lacking is us*. We are trying to fulfill our God-given mission in the world just as everyone has a God-given mission. We do this very imperfectly, but we press forward. "Not that I have already attained this or am already perfect, but I press on to make it my own, because Christ Jesus made me His own." (Philippians 3:12-14)

As mentioned in the *Hierarchy of Values* chapter, we put God first in our lives. This means living a Eucharistic life, including *daily* Mass, frequent visits to Christ in the Blessed Sacrament, weekly confession, and an integral daily prayer life. Does this have anything to do with formation of children? It has everything to do with it. *Without God's grace all of our practical ideas and methods would come to naught.*

Servant of God John Paul II exhorted in his *Letter to Families* (Article 18), "The Eucharist is truly a wondrous sacrament. In it Christ has given us himself as food and drink, as a source of saving power. He has left himself to us that we might have life and have it in abundance (cf. John 10:10): the life which is in him and which he has shared with us by the gift of the Spirit in rising from the dead on the third day. The life that comes from Christ is a life for us. It is for you, dear husbands and wives, parents, and families! Did Jesus not institute the Eucharist in a family-like setting during the Last Supper? When you meet for meals and are together in harmony, Christ is close to you. And he is Emmanuel, God with us, in an even greater way whenever you approach the table of the Eucharist. It can happen, as it did at Emmaus, that he is recognized only in "the breaking of the bread." (cf. Luke 24:35) It may well be that he is knocking at the door for a long time, waiting for it to be opened so that he can enter and eat with us (cf. Rev 3:20). The Last Supper and the words he spoke there contain all the power and wisdom of the sacrifice of the Cross. No other power and wisdom exist by which we can be saved and through which we can help to save others. There is no other power and no other wisdom by which you, parents, can educate both your children and yourselves. The educational power of the Eucharist has been proved down the generations and centuries."

For us, our entire lives center on the Eucharist. This means attending *daily* Mass, every day, and every one of us. We can't emphasize this enough. *Everything else is secondary*. And we attend *daily* Mass as an entire family, even the littlest toddlers and infants. Infinite graces *radiate* from Christ in the Eucharist into the souls of our littlest children, even when they are too young to receive the Body and Blood of Christ.

And we pray. The more one prays, the more one wants to pray, and the more strength and tenacity he has to continue to pray. We could say the same about living a Eucharistic life. One needs only to begin, make a little effort, and *God himself takes over*. "It is all God's work." (2 Corinthians 5:18)

Yes, we can see that family life is challenging, regardless of its size. We will not deceive you by saying that our family life is always ideal and tranquil. *Our family has plenty of faults to work on*. But we know that without Christ we could do nothing! We prefer to put our trust in him, not to try to go it alone. By his grace we humble ourselves to be "… like a sensible man who built his house on rock. Rains came down, floods rose, gales blew, and hurled themselves against that house and it did not fall: it was founded on rock." (Matthew 7:24-26)

Yes, his power is made perfect in our weakness. (Cf 2 Corinthians 12:9) And he will never leave us desolate. (Cf John 14:18) *We cannot raise our families on a starvation diet. We must pray, we must breathe the air of prayer*. And for Catholics, we need to *feed on Christ in the Eucharist <u>daily</u>*. *Don't be afraid. Be brave. God is with us. He is in command, and he loves us infinitely. With him we are invincible.*

Chapter 9

Called to Service

"Be strong, stand firm; be fearless, be dauntless and set to work, because Yahweh God, my God, is with you. He will not fail you, or forsake you before you have finished all the work to be done for the house of Yahweh."

(1 Chronicles 18:20)

Our responsibility as parents in forming our children is to be able to provide them with roots and with wings. They need to be able to make their faith their own, to be strong enough to venture forth and not be at the mercy of the whims and temptations of the world, to stand fast and to be a witness of the light and love of Christ to those in their path.

Now that several of our children are old enough to have left home, we have been blessed to see that they have indeed made their faith their own. We asked our oldest daughter, Shannon, during her first semester at college if she was still going to daily Mass. She appeared highly offended, and said "Of course!" Shannon currently attends a university to learn how to evangelize our society using today's technology and the media. Our second daughter, Tara, decided on her own initiative after graduating from high school to give the next year to Christ and others in service as an international volunteer coworker missionary. Our third daughter, Grace, spends time praying in front of abortion clinics with her college's pro-life group. Our fourth, fifth and sixth daughters, Colleen, Deirdre, and Bridget, have chosen to give Christ the first opportunity with their young lives by spending their high school years at a school far from home discerning a possible vocation to the consecrated life. Each of the oldest three has done the same as well. All of our daughters from age eleven have been very involved in service work with their peers through a Catholic girls club that aims to help girls see Christ as their best friend, and to challenge and transform the dominant culture for the better. Our first son, Shane, age twelve, is attending a minor seminary and feels God is calling him to become a priest, to give his life for Christ.

We have shared with you our philosophy on formation of children. But what is the ultimate goal of this formation? It is transformation, to become another Christ. This should be our goal as well as for our children. Through our baptismal call, each of us as children of God, are called to know, love, and serve God. *We are called to service.* We are called to be *witnesses of Christ's love* in the world. We are called to be his arms, his feet, his voice.

Some of the service work the children have been involved in over the years have been door-to-door missions, helping organize trips to museums and carnivals for poor inner city children, working to form younger children, delivering gifts to children in hospitals, visiting and entertaining the elderly in nursing homes, and praying and counseling as a family in front of abortions clinics.

Some ways that we have tried to live this vocation as lay adults is by offering ourselves in service at our parish, and by giving of our time and talents towards the faith formation of youth and adults on a larger scale as well.

This precious life we have been given on earth is not ours to do with as we will. We will be held accountable for the talents God entrusted to us. At the end of our lives, we will be judged not on what we accumulated in terms of money, power, prestige, or material possessions, but rather on how much we loved.

Contemplate how Christ loved us. Look to Christ, how he washed the feet of his apostles. We are called to *pour* ourselves out for others as Jesus Christ taught us by his example. "He then *poured* (emphasis added) water into a basin and began to wash the disciples' feet." (John 13:5) Christ *poured* everything out for love of us including every last drop of blood and water in his body. (Cf: John 19:35) He gave his very life for us so we may be with him forever. By the act of giving of ourselves sincerely and joyfully in service, we can imitate Christ. Through Christ, we can be Christ and bring Christ to others motivated only by love for souls and their eternal happiness. By the grace of God this will have a profound effect on any one with eyes to see. They will feel our love, which is God's love made manifest through us. Once we come to experience love through Christ, we can live love and be love, like Christ.

"This is my commandment: love one another as I have loved you. A man can have no greater love than to lay down his life for his friends." (John 15:12-13)

By his grace God has given the Littleton family the privilege of serving him and our fellow man. *Despite our many shortcomings*, he has *chosen* us. "You did not choose me, no, I chose you; and I commissioned you to go out and to bear fruit, fruit that will last." (John 15:16) *And he has chosen you!* What is he asking of you? You will find the answer in prayer.

We can only bear fruit when connected to the true vine, Christ, through prayer and for those who are Catholics, through the sacraments. (Cf: John 15:1-10) We must make our home in Christ and he will make his home in us. (Cf: John 15: 4) For cut off from Christ, we can do nothing, there will be no efficacy. (Cf: John 15:5)

So we must be confident in our mission. We are not alone in our efforts and work. There is no need for apprehension or fear. "Some hesitated." (Matthew 28:18) Yes, *God is with us!* "Know that I am with you always; yes, to the end of time." (Matthew 28:20)

Chapter 10

On the Cross

"I have branded you on the palms of my hands."
(Isaiah 49:16)

Like every person, like every family, we have experienced crosses in our lives (James). We do not claim that our crosses are the heaviest. We only know that they can be heavy for us, as yours are heavy for you. They have come in many shapes and forms for us. They have not been easy, but thanks to God, we have been consoled by the reality of *our crosses having a redemptive value*. In and of itself the cross would be worthless, a great loss, but the crosses and difficulties, crises, and disasters of our lives all have the capacity to bear much fruit, and culminate in our own growth and purification as well as in the overall redemption of mankind. "It makes me happy to suffer for you, as I am suffering now, and in my own body to do what I can to make up all that has still to be undergone by Christ for the sake of his body, the Church." (Colossians 1:24)

I share some of our crosses here in the hope that others will be encouraged that they are not alone in the experience of pain, sorrows, and difficulties in their lives. Being convinced of the good that comes from the cross consoles us, but does not take away the pain of the cross. The cross is exactly that, a cross.

In our family we have suffered the loss of five children through various stages of miscarriage, Maximilian Mary, Theresa Gerard, James Paul, Frances Xavier, and Joseph Faustina. Although these deaths have struck us deeply with sorrow, we are confident in the fact that this part of the Littleton team is in heaven, interceding for us and for others, as we complete our missions on earth.

Another cross has been the frequent fatigue and various degrees of sleep deprivation that Kathleen and I experience. I assume that most parents can relate to this. I personally find this a challenging part of life. Although we do our best to get enough rest, this often does not come about due to the many responsibilities that we have; but I will personally also admit that we should do better in achieving a balance with regard to needed rest.

On the Cross

A cross that we have often experienced is that of being judged harshly by others, even by those closest to us. We do our best to presume the best about others, that they have our best interests at heart, or perhaps have insufficient or incorrect information leading them to make a negative judgment about the way we lead our lives. It does help us to be involved with a good group of people with similar values as a means of encouragement and perseverance. Having been misjudged by others does afford us with an increased ability to fight against temptations to judge or speak negatively of others. When feeling offended by others it helps to remember the plank or better said the *redwood tree* in my own eye. (Cf: Luke: 6:41-42)

Then there is the difficulty of parting with our children when they have left home at an early age to embrace formation towards a possible priestly or consecrated vocation in the Catholic Church. Although their leaving home is difficult, we support our children because we want what is best for them, and we know that what is best for them is to follow God's will. This will make them happy in their lives here on earth as well as in eternity, and their lives will be most effective and fruitful by discerning and following our blessed Lord's will.

One of our most crushing crosses, which we pray will bear great fruit in the mystery of God's plan, is the financial crosses we have suffered. Back when our seventh child was six-weeks old, I quit my job and started an insurance adjusting business, knowing that it would be extremely difficult to make sufficient income working at a "job" for someone else. This started off reasonably well with God's help, but there were really only a couple years that we had surplus earnings. This business has been in decline for many years now.

I don't believe we ever had in our lives much more than ten thousand dollars in personal savings (other that the equity in our homes), and most of the time including now we have had nil in savings or close to it. For the most part during our married life, we have lived on the edge, often on the verge of financial disaster. We have never had much of a nest egg. Currently, our retirement savings are zero. We no longer have an IRA or 401K. As we write this book in August of 2006, we are actually facing the serious threat of bankruptcy and foreclosure. This is something we do not take lightly because of our moral values, in that we want to do all in our power to pay our creditors. Even if we were to go completely bankrupt, our intention is to go back and pay everything we owe to our creditors to the extent that we have the means to do so at some point in the future. We are literally facing the potential loss of our home and property. I suspect that if ever the worst happens we will end up with a roof over our heads somewhere, with our children being fed. (May, 2007 update: After many mysterious, providential twists and turns including a new job, we have evaded, but are still flirting with bankruptcy; and we still have a house over our heads, while we live a magnificent, but challenging adventure of trust in our Heavenly Father's good care.) Even in the highly improbable event we ever ended with the *cross* of being hungry and homeless, would that mean that we had made a mistake in cooperating with God to bring all of our children into the world? Of course not! *We can never reduce the value of the human person to economics.* Besides, when one believes in not only all that is seen, but also in all that is unseen/invisible (Cf: Nicene Creed) then the cross is no longer considered a failure. "Here are we preaching a crucified Christ... a Christ who is the power and wisdom of God. For God's foolishness is wiser than human wisdom, and God's weakness is stronger than human strength." (1 Corinthians 1:23-25)

"That is why there is no weakening on our part, and instead, though the outer man of ours may be falling into decay, the inner man is renewed day by day. Yes, the troubles that are soon over, though they weigh little, train us for the carrying of a weight of eternal glory that is out of all proportion to them. And so we have no eyes for things that are visible, but only for things that are invisible; for visible things last only for a time, and the invisible things are eternal." (2 Corinthians 16-18)

"If they experienced punishment as men see it, their hope was rich with immortality; slight was their affliction, great will their blessings be. God has put them to the test and proved them worthy to be with him, he has tested them like gold in a furnace, and accepted them as a holocaust. When the time comes for his visitation they will shine out; as sparks run through the stubble, so will they." (Wisdom 3:4-7)

I know without a shadow of a doubt that God is with us, he is in command, and that all will work out for the good and his glory, even as this involves some passing suffering and troubles for us. *What a great opportunity it is to recognize our dependency on God*, and to grow in trust in him. "Jar of meal shall not be spent, jug of oil shall not be emptied, before the day when Yahweh sends rain on the face of the earth." (1 Kings 17:14)

In the past few years it seems that everything that I have tried in terms of my business, including trying new business pursuits, has failed. I know that I have been doing everything in my control to make prudent decisions with regard to business and family, but with negative results. As long as I can know that I have done my part in doing my best to provide for my family, then I see the difficulties and failures as graces that God has given us.

Every cross is a tremendous grace, a gift from God. *It is when all appears lost, when we are put in an impossible situation that our faith deepens and we learn to depend on God totally.* This does not mean that we do not have to do our part. We must, and we do, but we know that ultimately God is in command, and is providentially arranging the events and circumstances of our lives for our good.

Through our crosses we learn to develop the *supernatural outlook* we need. God is in control. Things will not always go the way we prefer. We must learn to embrace all the circumstances of our lives, the pleasant and the difficult. We are called to be like Abraham, believing, totally confident in Almighty God, stepping out in blind trust. As difficult as our crosses have been, it is in a very real sense, liberating to be in an impossible situation where we have learned to put everything in God's hands and to trust him. God can and will bring good out of everything he permits.

It is when we receive the gift of being in a situation without a human solution that we really learn to surrender to God. He wants our total detachment from creatures, things, and our sense of control. This is an indispensable means to achieve intimacy with Christ. He wants to be our *All*.

It is when we are placed in a seemingly hopeless situation that we can learn to really *live one day at a time, to live in the moment, with peace and assurance that since God created us, he will sustain us*. We need to take the Lord at his word when he tells us, "Do not worry about tomorrow; tomorrow will take care of itself. Each day has enough trouble of its own." (Matthew 6:33-34)

Because of the grand gift of the cross God has permitted in our lives, we have learned to approach life like a marathon. I have run two marathons in my life. I never trained as thoroughly as I should have, so I hit the wall early. "Hitting the wall" is a phenomenon that happens when a runner feels he cannot run anymore, that he has met his limit. A marathon is twenty-six and two-tenths miles in distance. I think it is commonly understood that most runners hit the wall at about twenty miles, but for me it was at about sixteen miles. It was overwhelming to think that I had ten miles left to run since I felt that I was already spent, that I had already met my limit.

This is how it can be with the crosses in our lives. We think that our merciful Lord has perhaps made a mistake and permitted a cross that was beyond our capacity. But he knows us better than we know ourselves and what is best for us. "The trials that you have had to bear are no more than people normally have. You can trust God not to let you be tried beyond your strength, and with any trial he will give you a way out of it and the strength to bear it." (1 Corinthians 10:13)

So, when I hit the wall in the marathon, I convinced myself, "You can run just one more mile." One more mile seemed difficult, but did not seem as overwhelming as ten, so I was able to keep going. *We bring so much unnecessary anxiety down upon ourselves* by placing our entire future, days, months, and years ahead, on our shoulders. *God does not want us to do this* and he has told us so. "Do not worry about tomorrow." (Matthew 6:34)

So at seventeen miles, I made a deal with myself to run one more mile. Again it was arduous, but manageable. Eventually, even just one more mile was more than I could bargain for, more than I thought I could possibly do. So, I persuaded myself then that I could make it to one more street light. I would focus on running another one hundred feet to the streetlight, and then set a goal to run to the next street light. This way I completed the race.

I mentioned that I ran two marathons. The first time was more difficult because I make the mistake of periodically stopping running in order to rest. I gave in to the temptation to stop running and walked awhile. Once I walked, my entire body stiffened up. It became ten times more difficult to run. In some sense by giving in, by not consistently giving my personal best, by doubting, *by acquiescing to mediocrity, everything became much more difficult* than if I had just kept running. So the second time I ran a marathon, I ran the entire distance, and although it was very difficult and painful for me, it was much smoother than the year before when I rejected my cross of running, and gave into the mediocrity of walking.

I think of the example of my little daughter, Mairead, at age three, and the way that she embraced her little cross. Sweet, little Mairead was at regular morning Mass one day, standing on the kneeler, when suddenly she fell backwards hitting the back of her head on the sharp edge of a wooden chair. She ended up needing three or four stitches. She is one tough, positive, little girl. Initially she cried, which was one of those cries where over an extended time she silently sucked as much air into her lungs as possible, and then let out a deafening wail. After her initial short-lived cry, she did not cry again.

Later that morning, she obviously found her experiences at the hospital emergency room an intriguing and exciting adventure. While waiting to get stitches, I promised Mairead a prize if she didn't cry. I also bet one dollar with my daughter Maura, age eight, who accompanied us to the hospital, that Mairead would not cry. While waiting for the doctor to come in and stitch up the back of her head, Mairead sat up, leaving a blood stained pillow on the bed, and began singing one of her favorite songs at length with a huge smile on her face, while pumping her arms in the air, "She's a grand old flag …".

I stepped out of the curtained room for a moment and came back to find Maura, in an attempt to win the bet, whispering that it was alright for Mairead to cry. Nonetheless, Mairead did not as much as whimper when she was stitched up. I won the bet, and spent it on ice cream for Mairead on the way home. Yes, we included Maura in on the ice cream.

When experiencing the cross *we need to have our eyes on eternity*. Our lives have more meaning than what we externally experience in this world up until the time of our death. We need to live with the awareness that time is short and that we will each die, but that on the other hand, our eternity is only beginning then. *We are building our eternity with the lives that we live here on earth*. This world in its present form is not our final destination. We are strangers and sojourners here. So many people frustrate themselves believing or at least living as if their lives on earth were the sole purpose of their existence, trying to make their heaven now on earth. Yes, in a sense, it *can* be heaven on earth when we unite ourselves with God and his will. We will only be completely happy when united with God and this can and does *begin* on earth, when we make God our Everything, when we completely give Him our heart. We need to live for God first, like St. Paul, "I have been crucified with Christ, and I live now not with my own life but with the life of Christ who lives in me." (Galatians 2:19)

We have to allow our crosses, difficulties, and impossible situations to unite us more closely to God. We need to embrace our crosses. We cannot be like those who taunted Christ, "Come down from the cross now for us to see it and believe." (Mark 15:32) Rather, we need to live like St. Paul who said, "During my stay with you the only knowledge I claimed to have was about Jesus, and only about Him as the crucified Christ." (1 Corinthians 2:2-3)

The cross, sorrow, pain is sanctifying and *anoints with maturity and wisdom*. God uses pain: physical, moral, mental, emotional, and especially interior suffering to purify and prepare us for our mission in life, and to draw us closer to him for all eternity. "And there was one that wrestled with him until daybreak who seeing that he could not master him, struck him in the socket of his hip, and Jacob's hip was dislocated as he wrestled with him. He said, 'Let me go for day is breaking'. But Jacob answered, 'I will not let you go until you bless me.' He then asked, 'What is your name?' 'Jacob', he replied. He said, your name shall no longer be Jacob, but Israel, because you have been strong against God, you shall prevail against men.'… And he blessed him there. Jacob named the place Peniel, 'Because I have seen God face to face,' he said 'and I have survived.' The sun rose as he left Peniel, limping because of his hip… he had struck Jacob in the socket of the hip on the sciatic nerve." (Genesis 32:26-32) It was only through the means of pain, of the cross, that Jacob was able to see God *face to face*, receive his blessing, and be purified for his great mission, a mission so great that it even required a great name change. To be named Israel is akin to being named Christ, because the people of Israel prefigured the Church, which is the *mystical body* of Christ. We are all called to cooperate with God's purifying, sanctifying action to be transformed into other Christs.

As anyone who has ever experienced sciatic nerve pain can attest to, it is exceptionally painful. It *cost*

Jacob a lot of pain to be transformed into Israel, a prefigurement of Christ. It is through the cross, prayer, and for Catholics, the sacraments, that we *wrestle* the graces we need from God. It is then that the sun comes up in our existence. The rising of the sun, the resurrection, comes only after the cross; and we can count on the fact that the cross is always followed by the resurrection, as long as we do not purposely impede God's plan.

When we really exercise faith, when we allow God to transform us through our crosses, we become *invincible*, fearless; we receive peace. We know that everything will turn out for the good. "I believe nothing can happen that will outweigh the supreme advantage of knowing Christ Jesus, my Lord. For Him, I have accepted the loss of everything and look on everything as so much rubbish if only I can have Christ…." (Philippians 3:8-9)

Why are we *invincible*? Because we rely on God! We are one with him. Only he is invincible. *When we rely on ourselves alone, we are setting ourselves up for major shock and disappointment.* Despite all our crosses in the Littleton family, Kathleen and I know that God can provide for us and for our fourteen children as easily as he can for families with one or two. " 'They may put their trust in their weapons and their exploits,' he said, ' but our confidence is in Almighty God, who is able with a nod to overthrow both those marching on us and the whole world with them.' " (2 Maccabees 8:18)

God is love. Everything he does is out of love for us. So why be afraid? I am a black belt in the martial art of Kenpo, and *supposedly* a somewhat tough guy in that respect. But the truth is that before I had faith, I was afraid of many things. Now, with God, at least deep within my interior, I am afraid of nothing - that is, *as long as I remain focused and grounded in Christ, grounded in prayer and the sacraments.*

Another severe cross has been the activity of the demonic in our lives. Demons do exist. This is a doctrine of the Christian faith. However, many have fooled themselves into thinking that the reality of demons and their activity in our lives is just a myth. This is a dangerous deception. One proof of the existence and activity of the demonic to me is in so many educated, highly intelligent people who believe ridiculous things such as the argument that a baby being killed in a partial birth abortion or any abortion for that matter is not really a human being yet, and that abortion can somehow be justified. *What*? Here is what Christ said about the devil: "He was a murderer from the start; he was never grounded in the truth; there is not truth in him at all, when he lies he is drawing on his own store, because he is a liar, and the father of lies." (John 8:44)

By the way, I am a firm believer that whenever the evils of abortions are discussed, the truth must be proclaimed about God's infinite mercy and readiness to forgive those who have had or aided in abortions.

Satan will tempt us to sin, and try to convince us that something is not a sin. Then when we have fallen and committed the sin, he switches tactics, and tempts us towards despair trying to convince us that the sin is so horrible that it cannot be forgiven, that God has rejected us, that we are worthless, that it is not even worth trying to be good. But Jesus Christ is *Mercy*. He is always ready to forgive. We can always count on God's help. "Go and learn the meaning of the words, *What I want is mercy, not sacrifice.* And indeed I did not come to call the virtuous, but sinners." (Matthew 9:13)

I think that anyone who is sincerely trying to live a prayerful, good life and to follow God's will, upon close consideration can attest to some manifestation of the demonic in his or her life. It is generally those who depend not on God, but on themselves, following their own will and not God's will, that claim not to be harassed by the demonic. This is because the devil is highly intelligent, and prefers stealth. It is when the devil has, through covertness, been highly effective and has a soul exactly where he wants him, that he remains hidden and *seems* to leave the soul at peace. *But there are no peace treaties with Satan*, only one-sided false treaties which he will never honor, but only take advantage of and leverage against us. The devil wants to destroy every single human being created in God's image and likeness. The devil hates you, and wants to kill you, destroy you, and every member of your family with you. No person, *by himself*, is any match for Satan's far superior power and intelligence.

Having personally encountered crushing demonic assaults in our lives, we can assure you that the devil's evilness and hatred are beyond words to describe. He has made it known that he does not like this book. Having said this, *we have nothing whatsoever to fear from the devil when we place ourselves under the protection of Jesus Christ.* This is the key. When we do not place ourselves under Christ's protection, we have everything to fear.

The devil can assault us in many ways. One ordinary way is through temptation, through thoughts and images he places or recalls in our minds and imagination. We should never, never engage the demonic in dialogue, or we are setting ourselves up for a *fall*. That is how it started in the Garden of Eden. (Cf: Genesis 3) When temptations come we should not entertain them, but *immediately pray* and get our mind and activities focused on something else. It is important to know and remember that the devil cannot force us to sin. God never permits the devil to control our free will. We always retain this gift. Our will needs to be merged with God's will. This happens through prayer, and for those of us who are Catholic, especially through the sacraments, mixed with our sacrifices and efforts.

Satan tries to sow doubts and distrust of our Blessed Lord, because this is the opposite of the faith and trust that God asks of us which unites us safely to him, and brings us true peace. "Did God really say you were not to eat from any of the trees in the garden?" (Genesis 3:1-2) As in this case, the devil also will often use a partial truth to disguise a lie and temptation. God never said they could not eat of *any* of the trees. He only specified *one* tree. God had actually said, "You may eat indeed of all the trees in the garden. Nevertheless of the tree of the knowledge of good and evil you are not to eat, for on the day you eat of it you shall surely die." (Genesis 2:16-17)

Our poor mother, Eve, entered into dialogue with the devil and failed to seek God's help, and to trust in him. In addition to pride, this is why she fell. In my opinion another reason Eve fell is that *Adam did not fulfill his role as spiritual head of the family, and he failed to protect her. We men need to pay attention to this.* Adam also sinned and ate of this forbidden tree. But God is able to bring good out of everything. He gave us the Blessed Virgin Mary to be the new Eve, and he himself took human flesh to become the new Adam, and redeem the fallen human race. We now have more than we ever lost through original sin. To quote the Catholic Church's Easter vigil liturgy: "O happy fault, O necessary sin of Adam, which gained for us so great a Redeemer!"

Another way the devil manifests himself is through agitation. For example, a family may decide that they want to begin praying nightly, and then they find that arguments, agitation, haste, and disorder break out in the family. When this happens, the family should not be deterred in the least, but rather turn to God with a greater trust and sense of dependency. Regardless of temptations, disruptions, and distractions we must always persevere in doing God's will in whatever good he wants us to carry out. With God's help we will prevail through these difficulties in the end.

Other manifestations are feelings of overwhelming anxiety and temptations towards despair. The devil does everything possible to try to erode and destroy our faith, hope, and trust in God. When this happens, we need to immediately recognize this as the temptation that it is and pray and seek God's protection. We should never try to do battle with the demonic on our own. We must always turn to Jesus Christ, and when we do, we can count on always being protected and helped. We may still be assaulted and tempted, but the devil will never prevail against Jesus Christ. Of this we can be certain. *No matter how terrible the storm, we are safe with Christ.* Even when it appears Christ is asleep in the boat, he is still in command and can calm a storm with a word, with a glance. "Even the wind and the sea obey

Him." (Mark 4:41) We must have faith. *With faith we are invincible, because we are one with God.*

Another great means of protection from demonic assaults and temptation is invoking the Blessed Virgin Mary as well as St. Michael the Archangel though prayer. "The woman brought a male child into the world, the son who was to rule all he nations with an iron scepter, and the child was taken straight up to God and to his throne, while the woman escaped into the desert, where God had made a place of safety ready... And now war broke out in heaven, when Michael with his angels attacked the dragon. The dragon fought back with his angels, but they were defeated and driven out of heaven. The great dragon, the primeval serpent, known as the devil or Satan, who had deceived all the world, was hurled down to the earth and his angels were hurled down with him. Then I heard a shout from heaven, 'Victory and power and empire forever have been won by our God, and all authority for his Christ, now that the persecutor, who accused our brothers day and night before our God, has been brought down. They have triumphed over him by the blood of the Lamb, and by the witness of their martyrdom, because even in the face of death they would not cling to life. Let the heavens rejoice and all who live there; but for you, earth and sea, trouble is coming- because the devil has gone down to you in a rage, knowing that his days are numbered.'" (Revelation 12:5-12)

May we not be deceived along with the world. If we are to be protected from the devil's rage we must place ourselves with confidence under the security and protection of the Blood of the Lamb, Christ Jesus. Like the martyrs we must live by a true and sure *hierarchy of values*, where we place God and his will before all things, no matter the cost. *There is a war going on.* There is no use denying it. *We are in it up to our necks*, but we are assured of victory, if we only avail ourselves of the *superior firepower available to us*, the ultimate weapon, Christ and his grace.

We can even look at the temptations, agitations, and attempts at destroying family unity and peace, at destroying the very institution of the family itself, that the devil assaults us with as a gift, as an opportunity. Even this is a cross that we can embrace and offer back to God through our prayers and efforts to overcome and persevere through these assaults with his help. These assaults become a *battlefield on which we can gain merit and demonstrate our love for God*. God can and does bring good even out of this. When we are assaulted and tempted by the demonic *we learn how little, how powerless we are, and how truly dependent we are on God.* This can be a means of acquiring the *indispensable virtue of humility.*

Another tactic the devil uses is to turn the things to which we are attached against us and against our faith. That is why we cannot be attached to anything but God himself. Yes, we can use the things God has blessed us with, for the good purpose they were created for, for our good and for God's glory, but we cannot give our hearts to these things. *We must have a holy, supernatural detachment.*

Remember in scripture where Jesus Christ reached the country of the Gerasenes and he cast the legion of unclean spirits out of the man and they asked for leave to go into the herd of two thousand pigs? They then "charged down the cliff into the lake and there they were drowned." (Mark 5:13) What did these pigs mean to the people in the town and country around there? Obviously they meant a great deal, and the legion of demons *knew it.* They probably were important to the economy of these people. These two thousand pigs were a real loss to them, but unfortunately the demons were successful in their ruse at least for the time being, in that the people there valued these pigs, of all things *pigs,* more than they valued Jesus Christ. They implored him to leave the neighborhood. They told him to get out. They drove their peace, faith, and hope away in the person of Jesus Christ our Lord, due to their attachments. Perhaps God is telling us through this scripture that each of our attachments are nothing more than *pigs* compared to him. How can we trade our All, God himself for the *pigs* in our lives?

Fortunately Christ was able to bring good as he always does, even out of this fiasco, as he loves us infinitely and never gives up on us. "We know that by turning everything to their good God co-operates with all those who love him, with all those that he has called according to his purpose." (Romans: 8:28) He sent the man whom he drove the legion of demons out to "'tell them all that the Lord in His mercy has done for you'. So the man went off and proceeded to spread throughout the Decapolis all that Jesus had done for him. And everyone was amazed". (Mark 5:19-20) In the long run many people came to Christ as a result of this confrontation he had with the demonic. To borrow an idea from Servant of God, Archbishop Fulton Sheen, *the devil has his hour, but God has his day.* (Cf: *Life of Christ*, page 328)

Out of love for us God does permit us to be tested. *We can really only show love when it costs us something, through sacrifice.* Many know the story of Job, how God permitted Satan to assault him, how Job lost everything including his property, possessions, children, and health. He questioned God in a long conversation about this, but in the end, he *surrendered*. He had been transformed through the cross, through sorrow, through the experience of Christ. *It was only through the cross that he came to know and be one with God.* "I know that you are all-powerful; what you conceive you can perform. I am the man who obscured your designs with my empty-headed words. I have been holding forth on matters I cannot understand, marvels beyond me and my knowledge…. I knew you then only by hearsay; but now, *having seen you with my own eyes*, I retract all I have said, and in dust and ashes I repent." (Job 42:2-6) Like Jacob it took the cross to bring Job *face to face* with God.

Once Job was transformed, he was capable of being another Christ, capable of interceding for and helping God to redeem others. Yahweh was angry however with

Job's three advisors and directed them to go to Job to offer a holocaust, while Job, his servant, offered prayers for them. These men had not yet had the experience of the cross. Job, purified by the cross, was able to successfully intercede for them.

It was then that Yahweh listened to Job with favor, "Yahweh restored Job's fortunes, because he had prayed for his friends. More than that, Yahweh gave him double what he had before." (Job 42:10-11)

The world is being redeemed through the cross. As truly difficult as our crosses are, it is a great privilege to be given the gift of crosses in our lives. *There is one thing we will not have in heaven that we will have great nostalgia for, and that is the ability to suffer through, with, and in Christ by bearing our crosses for him and with him here on earth. The cross is literally joined to God.* God let himself be nailed to the cross. If we want to be one with God here on earth, we need to *let him pull us up on the cross with him,* because in a real sense that is where he is at, that is where we find him. *We can only really see the world for what it is through the view from up on the cross. We learn to love everything and every one from the cross, because God is love, and he is one with the cross.*

Sure, Christ died once, rose, and is seated at the right hand of the Father in heaven, but he is mystically still on the cross through his *mystical body*, the Church ... through you and through me. This truth is also fundamental to the mystery of why you and I are one in Christ's *mystical body*. We are up there on the cross together. We are one with Christ, and we are *invincible* there. The cross leads to the resurrection. Christ is with us. We just need to be faithful and not tell Christ to get out of the neighborhood of our soul. With him we are utterly secure; without him we are lost.

Paraphrasing Servant of God, Archbishop Fulton Sheen by memory from an unrecalled source, let us be consoled by the fact that *Christ never once mentioned his cross without also speaking of the resurrection*. And as long as we don't reject him, and we do God's will, we will be resurrected and saved so we can be one with Jesus Christ for all eternity, the *bridegroom* fully consummating his love with His *bride*, the Church, including you and me.

Chapter 11
The Importance of Having a Sense of Humor

"Here we are fools, for the sake of Christ while you are the learned men…"

(1 Corinthians 4:10)

I'm (Kathleen) sure it happens to moms and dads who have three or more children. It sure happens to us all the time. The normal parameters of common courtesy seem to disintegrate. People who see us with three or more of our children in tow feel compelled to break the norms of polite conversation and say the craziest things to us!

A few examples of some crazy things people say to us in public places like grocery store lines or at playgrounds are: "Thought that went out with high button shoes? Do you know what causes that? You should get a TV!"

Way back when we had only four or five children some of these surprising and unexpectedly rather rude questions would tend to upset me as the mom. As we continued to have more children, I became far less sensitive, and rather came to expect such comments. I even prepared myself with lighthearted comebacks that also may serve to plant a seed.

Some of my responses go like this: "Are these all your children?" "No, I left a bunch at home! Really, I'm not kidding."

"Wow, do you have help?" "No, are you offering? Seriously, no, we don't have help, we help each other."

"Are you going to have more?" "I don't know, only God knows. It's really up to him. I'm just open to what he wants, and that way I know I'll never have any regrets for not having the children God intended me to have. I see it as a great grace, privilege, and blessing that he would entrust to me the care and formation of an eternal soul."

"You have that many and they are so well-behaved ... I have only one and I can barely manage!" "It's easier than you may think! In a large family, the children have each other and don't need the mom for their sole source of attention and entertainment. Also jobs are shared so that the mom and dad don't have to do everything ... many hands make light work. The children learn responsibility, generosity, patience, and sharing from an early age, and that life isn't all about 'me'."

"Fourteen children, wow, how do you do it?" "Well, they came along just one at a time. We didn't wake up one day to discover we had fourteen children! It's our life and so it doesn't seem so extraordinary."

I'm often surprised when other people are so surprised by us. We take one day at a time, putting God first. He created us and he will sustain us. He intends only the best for us and we trust in him.

I have also experienced some rather unusual and humorous reactions from people who just don't seem to be able to grasp the fact that we do indeed have fourteen living children. Literally, I've witnessed people's mouths drop open in shock and they are seized with a type of temporary paralysis when they hear that I am the mother of fourteen. Once they recover, all normality in the conversation ceases and suddenly they want to know every detail of my life ... from did they all come out of my body ... to what size car do I drive ... to how many bathrooms do we have ... to what does my husband do for a living.

Sometimes we have to go to extraordinary lengths to convince people that yes, indeed the children are all ours, and yes, there are fourteen of them living. A few years ago we moved to a new town and wanted to join the community pool for the summer. The pool staff didn't believe that the sixteen people I was registering were all part of my immediate family. I had to give them references of existing pool members who could attest to the fact that the fourteen children I was trying to register were really mine and not neighbor kids that I was trying to sneak in on our family membership!

The Illinois Department of Revenue in 2002 and in 2007 and the IRS in 2006 audited us, challenging the number of exemptions shown on our return. The Illinois Department of Revenue merely required a full list of dependents and their social security numbers. The IRS had our children's accurate names and social security numbers, however, challenged their existence anyway in a somewhat drawn out process. In both cases we have of course, won out, because our children REALLY DO EXIST!

It usually happens that when Jim comes to visit me and a brand new baby in the hospital with all the kids, he has had to sneak past the nurse's station as he always gets stopped, and they contest whether or not the children with him are all siblings of the new baby ...

The Importance of Having a Sense of Humor

thinking he's sneaking in non-family members! Like we really need any one else to tag along!

When one of the older daughters is holding a baby in an airport or an elevator, it has happened that someone will think she is the baby's mom … recently someone wished my thirteen-year-old a happy mother's day! People don't seem able to comprehend the fact that our children are spread out over a twenty-year period of time and yes, I'm the mom that's still having the babies.

Jim, as the father, has his own way of dealing with the crazy things people say to him. In his words: "When asked, 'Are these all your children?' being the ham I am with the reactions of people, I will usually say something like, 'These are all my children, but they are not *ALL* my children.' When I get the hoped for look of confusion, I then explain that each of the children with me are in fact my children, but that there are many more where these came from. Then I will smoothly fit into the conversation that I have nineteen children, fourteen living and five in heaven, and then deal more seriously with whatever comments are made at that time."

(Kathleen) We really look at these as opportunities for evangelization both with regard to the wonders and desirability of having a large family, but also of our faith in God and his certain providential care for us. More often than not people will often question our ability to monetarily or otherwise provide for our large family. This is a great opportunity which we generally seize upon to speak of the grace we have received of a deep and confident trust in the good providential care of our heavenly Father and that he is in command and capable of providing for our needs. God created us and he will sustain us!

A sense of humor is indispensable in life. Our blessed Lord gave it to us for a reason. It is a great gift that we should utilize and not annihilate. One way to nurture this gift is by not taking ourselves overly seriously all the time. Here Jim shares some humorous and unusual situations that have occurred to us over the years.

I remember being on a cruise ship when Tara, our second child, was one-year-old. When we woke up in the morning, I looked over at Tara in her bed. She was of course wearing diapers. It appeared to me that somehow she had gotten a hold of a large quantity of chocolate candy and had literally painted herself and the walls around her bed with it. I asked Kathleen as she was waking up, "Who gave Tara the chocolate?" *That is when the odor hit me.* It became apparent that during the night (yes, we can sleep through anything) Tara's diaper had erupted like a massive volcano spewing "number two" all over the wall and her bed. Due to the fact that we were on a cruise ship, we did not have access to the materials necessary to clean up a potty disaster of this enormity. Kathleen bathed Tara, dressed her, and as we left the cabin I ran into the cabin steward. I told him apologetically that my daughter had had an accident, and that there was a significant mess to be cleaned up in the cabin. I seem to recall that I also told him the nature of the mess. The steward flippantly and confidently chuckled and said that it was not uncommon for him to deal with matters such as this in his experience. I told him that he had certainly *never* dealt with *anything like this* before. When we came back to the cabin, sure enough it was clean, but that poor man had put a major dent in his purgatory.

There was an earlier occasion when our eldest, Shannon, was about ten-months-old. We were on a trip to Florida, and had gone to lunch at Fuddruckers, a popular retro hamburger place. Shannon had a similar experience with her diaper erupting all over her and the highchair. (No, despite these stories, our children do not suffer from chronic intestinal problems.) We did not have the means to clean it up, and had left the diaper bag back at the hotel. This was before my reversion, and I did not exercise the charity of telling the staff about the mishap, so some unfortunate employee later undoubtedly encountered the very unpleasant surprise when he went to clean up the chair at our table. In retrospect I only hope that he noticed what was on the chair before unexpectedly wiping it down with a rag.

The saga continued, and when we arrived back at the hotel, Shannon was literally covered with "number two" from head to toe. My workouts and reasonably good physical condition paid off in a way I had never imagined in that I had the strength and ability to hold Shannon at arms length in front of me as I walked. As we entered the hotel lobby, to our horror, we found ourselves in the midst of a large wedding party including the bride. We had no choice but to make our way weaving in between them. Fortunately we did not bump Shannon into anyone as we passed through the throng. I hope we did not make it into the wedding pictures.

Perhaps my favorite potty story is a time when we were shopping for Halloween costumes at a department store when our fourth oldest daughter, Colleen, was on the cusp of being potty trained. She was sitting in the seat in the shopping cart. We had all of our children with us at the time. We were pushing the cart through the costume aisle that was scattered with costumes that had been strewn on the floor. Colleen told us that she had to go potty. We asked her to hold off for a minute, but she didn't. We discovered to our mortification that she urinated as we were pushing the cart through and over the various costumes on the floor. This was before my reversion as well, and my personal sense of truthfulness was quite broadminded. I told Kathleen that we had the duty (good start, but bad finish) to let the store personnel know so that customers would not come along and unknowingly pick up and purchase the urine-saturated costumes.

So I went and found a store employee about fifty-feet away where I could still see my family standing guilty at the scene of the misdeed. Pointing towards my family, I said to this employee, "I want to make you aware that *someone's* child just urinated all over the Halloween costumes on the floor over there." He responded, "You're kidding!" "No, really," I said. "That's gross," he said. I agreed with him and said he should probably get someone over to clean up the mess. Rationalizing that it was irrelevant, I never owned up to the fact this it was my daughter who was the culprit. Besides, if I revealed that it was my daughter, he might have asked that I be the one to clean up the mess.

We have had many rather interesting experiences while traveling with our large family. In 2002, we traveled as a family to a religious convention in Baltimore, Maryland where our family could receive formation to grow in holiness and to be of better service to our Blessed Lord and others. We had two rooms in a hotel, but with twelve children at the time, that meant seven persons per room. Hotels generally have their rules about a maximum of four per room. I must admit that when they don't ask, we don't tell how many people are in our family. (Our moral reasoning is that hotel rules of this nature do not reasonably and justly provide for large families, due to the fact that they are woefully too uncommon today). So our normal mode of operation is that after registering, we either bring the family in a back door, or when we have to pass the desk in the lobby, we enter in two or three smaller groups so as not to tip off the hotel personnel as to the size of our family and the numbers staying in our rooms. When we use the pool, we suspect that the hotel staff must think we have invited friends over and are having a big party.

When we arrived in Baltimore, we discovered that the downtown hotel we were staying at did not have any parking facility available for our oversized fifteen-passenger van pulling a luggage trailer behind. So, after unloading the family and our many possessions for the weeklong trip, I asked the doorman about parking, and he suggested that I go to the major league baseball stadium a few blocks away where I would find parking for oversized vehicles. Firstly, as it turned out he was mistaken that there was any parking available there for my van and trailer. Secondly, he did not tell me that there was a major league baseball game getting under way there with massive traffic.

In a strung out, exhausted state from our drive halfway across the country, I naively followed the man's advice and ended up driving the van and trailer through a gate and into a huge, packed baseball stadium parking lot. Cars were so packed in there that it would have been difficult enough to maneuver a compact car down the aisles, and here I was with my fifteen-seat van pulling the trailer. This is when I learned from the attendant that they did in fact not allow for oversized parking.

I quickly realized I had made a colossal poor judgment by entering this parking lot, and that I needed to get out of it; but the only way out was to continue forward and to drive though various aisles to get around to the exit. This required many sharp, tight turns. These turns appeared physically impossible for my van and trailer. Of course there quickly developed a line of cars with impatient drivers waiting behind me. There was no going back. I was envisioning being stuck there indefinitely, not being able to maneuver myself out, and with no one else being able to move in or out of the parking lot due to the growing traffic jam that I had created behind me.

In the long run, somehow, inexplicably, I was able to negotiate the turns, missing cars literally by a fraction of an inch, repeatedly backing up and going forward to squeeze my van and trailer through the various turns and out of this parking lot. I cannot express what a relief it was when the van and trailer finally burst out into the freedom of the street beyond this lot. But I was mentally and physically exhausted by the experience.

Eventually, I was able to find a parking lot on the outskirts of town that did accept oversize vehicles such as mine. This lot had not been mentioned by the doorman. Although I would have loved nothing more than to wring the doorman's neck, when I finally dragged myself back to the hotel, by the grace of God, I calmly restrained myself and told him that he was incorrect in his parking suggestion and that he should be cautious about giving the same advice to other families with oversize vehicles in the future (as if he encounters a lot of them). Thanks to my keen perception I was able to glean that the doorman did not remember me, did not understand me, and did not really care about anything I was saying.

We stayed at this brand name relatively upscale hotel for four days and through some sort of a mix-up, despite our calls, not once during the entire four days were our rooms cleaned. I guess we received our payback for thinking we had gotten away with having so many people in two rooms! But aren't these bizarre and sometimes difficult experiences what make for enjoyable memories, *after much time* passes?

Sometimes humor is the only way to cope with the chaos that tends naturally to happen despite the best-laid plans. In March of 2006 our entire family was together including our newborn baby, so we made it a planned priority to take photos. My parents happened to be visiting so Kathleen handed the new baby, Shealagh Maeve, to my mom so she could hold her, so the rest of the family could assemble on the staircase for the taking of our family photographs. We took a number of photographs before we realized that the baby was not being included, even though her arrival was one of the main purposes of taking the photos in the first place! Imagine the disbelief and laughter when we realized that after all that hassle of getting the children to look just right in the photos, we realized we had to do it all over again, this time with the new baby included!

"Get the bucket" is a term I coined several years ago as a response to the frequent tears of certain children whose primary and emotive temperament caused them to cry copiously at the drop of a hat. The implication is that we will all be awash in tears if we don't get a bucket quickly to contain them. But no worries, as our daughter, Colleen, who the term was first used for at the age of four, has outgrown this proclivity, and is now a rock of a leader and good example at age seventeen.

I coined the phrase "step bread". This is based on the condition of the bread our family often consumes, because whenever we buy bread, someone tends to step on it and smash it in the van before we get it into the pantry.

Our sons use hair gel or tonic to help their hair stay neatly combed (which is part of their human formation). I came up with the term *hair grease* for these products. We will often tell the boys, "Get your hair greased," meaning they should groom their hair to look presentable. On one occasion when Patrick was five years old and getting a hair cut from a beautician, he told her that he had grease on his hair. She took this literally, and was grossed out until she was told that he meant hair gel, and not *hair grease*!

I coined the phrase "*Bopper*". This is connected to the term "*Teenie Bopper*," and while it is not fully representative of the point I make, I use the term "*bopper*" when I need to question and challenge the modesty level of one our girls' clothing, and my standards are strict. I'll say, uh oh, we don't have a *bopper* here do we? This brings some humor into the formation that I try to keep as positive as possible. I encourage my children to dress with modesty and dignity. For example, I motivate the girls by assuring them that there is nothing more beautiful than a modestly dressed, dignified young lady.

We have a system where we protect our children from the growing and flagrant immorality and decadence presented in the previews at movie theatres when we go to a carefully selected wholesome movie as a family. Normally we don't enter the theatre until the movie is beginning in order not be exposed to the previews. Recently in 2006, I took nine of the children to see the movie, *Cars*. It was going to be a crowded theatre, so as opposed to Plan A where none of our children would go inside the theatre until the feature film began, I executed Plan B wherein I sent two of the more mature children in to save ten seats, waiting with their heads bowed and eyes down and maintaining recollection and prayer so as to protect themselves from any decadence in the previews. They sat with eight seats in between them. The rest of the children waited outside in the lobby with me supervising. I went into the theatre to see if the movie was starting and I noticed a group of children go past my daughter who was sitting on the end, ignoring her charitable comments that she was saving those seats for our family. There were still plenty of other seats in the theatre for this smaller group, and I pointed out that these seats were being saved. The apparent father of these children asked how many seats we were saving, and I said ten. He reacted quite hostilely and indignantly and exclaimed, "Ten!" I acknowledged that he had heard correctly, and he reluctantly left us our seats. This is only an impression, but I think the poor man was unable to fathom the possibility that we might have a large enough family to require all these seats, and that he suspected that perhaps I was only trying to save extra seats so that we would have more elbow room. Imagine if I had brought the entire family!

We have a traditional family phrase for when we encounter pain, such as for example when one of the children sustain a cut or scrape. They will often say, "Pain, I love it!" Why? No, we are not sadists. We do not enjoy seeing a family member in pain. The reality of life, however, is that we all encounter pain in varying degrees from time to time. We are attempting to form our children in virtues like fortitude and tenacity so that we do not waste time and energy in life lamenting about pain and difficulties, but rather channel it to purify and strengthen our character, not to mention its transcendent value when offered spiritually for others.

Today there is a pill for everything. The dominant culture tells us that if there is any pain or difficulty, there is something amiss. We need to learn to embrace the pain which our good God permits in our lives. When pain, difficulties, and sorrows do not kill us, they make us stronger. Our country was not founded, developed, and made great by people who avoided pain and difficulty. Nothing was every achieved without passing through the crucible of pain and difficulties, even sorrow. Our armed forces still understand this and always will. Basic training will never be a comfortable experience, bereft of any pain. Soldiers are forged through pain, challenges, and difficulties. The more elite the soldier, the more painful and challenging will be his training.

We have a family warning phrase, "O O", which stands for "*Offended One*". When a family member is showing signs of having been offended, another family member, especially me, might say, "*O O*". This is the tip off that the family member needs to set aside the temptation to be offended, forgive, and move on. "*O O*" is an admonishment not to be an *offended one*.

A similar saying is "*Crush It.*" *Crush it* refers to crushing one's ego when it is manifesting itself through a self-centered or offended attitude. We have a standing rule in the family that pouting is never rewarded. At the first sign of a pout, mom, dad or an older sibling announces that, "Pouting is never rewarded!" Whatever the goal was for the pouting, the child quickly realizes that their tactic won't work and switches her or his demeanor.

Whenever we get into our fifteen-passenger van, we have one child, most recently Shane, designated to count to make sure we have everyone present. He then announces each individual's name to confirm their presence and that seatbelts are fastened. It is sort of like a pilot preparing an aircraft for takeoff. As Shane announces each person's name for seatbelt confirmation, the response has evolved into "Yes, sir, shoulder strap, sir." This confirms that not only the seatbelt portion is secure, but that the shoulder strap is also correctly positioned. He then announces to the driver that "Everyone is buckled, sir!" It is quite amusing to watch and listen to the children, even our one-year-old in her own way, efficiently and sharply rattling off this quasi-military exercise.

A recent new, fun, and formative family tradition has developed at the check out lines at grocery stores. Unfortunately there are many inappropriate magazines positioned there. We get the children's attention focused on unloading the grocery cart onto the conveyer belt and then move them quickly past the check out line to the exit area. The younger children then pretend to be a military unit where they all line up at attention. We often have a contest to see who can best stand quietly at attention. They really have a lot of fun with this and it also becomes quite entertaining to the people watching them in the store.

I have to admit that I am often as much of a ham with my family as was the father in the original *Cheaper by the Dozen* movie. And no, we are not imposing a militaristic dictatorship on our children. We are utilizing fun and imagination in forming, organizing, and protecting them, and in creating family unity. They love it.

Then when we leave the store, the children march single file doing their left faces and right faces as they progress to the van. Then a couple of the children are assigned to *inside duty* where they will receive the bags of food while inside the van from those children assigned *outside duty* who hand the bags into the van.

When we receive the personal service of a store employee carting the groceries to the van, we always give him a tip. That responsibility is given to one of the children who gives the tip once the bags are loaded. The goal is that mom or dad doesn't have to touch a thing, but merely oversee, and that everything happens quickly and in an organized fashion. This is a great means of having fun, establishing teamwork, unity, discipline, and industriousness.

Another one of our family traditions is singing when we travel in our van or car. We have various songs, but one in particular is the song from the old John Wayne western, *She Wore a Yellow Ribbon*. We changed the word *lover* to *husband* in the song to make it family appropriate. The song is triggered by me saying in a prolonged booming, militaristic voice, "Forward!" and the children immediately respond in unison, "HO!" at which time they start singing the song with vocalized instrumentals and the words in two part harmony. This never fails to cheer up and revitalize the family.

Some additional family games and activities are as follows. As a motivating factor to be ready on time to get to daily Mass we use the reward of throwing the football outside the church before going in. Everyone is included from dad on down to the youngest child.

We always plan for the unexpected by allowing more time than we need to get ready in the morning so that we can still arrive to church on time. And something unexpected always happens! One of the children usually can't find their shoes, and we have on occasion gone to church with one child in stocking feet. Programming extra time for the *expected unexpected* is the key to arriving anywhere in a timely way.

(Kathleen) Someone once told us very seriously and with the best of intentions, "You know it's not just about having babies, you have to raise them you know." Really, did they think we weren't aware of that! Maybe they thought a new baby to us is like getting a puppy is to a child … it would just stay small and cute and huggable and not come with any responsibility! Yes, raising a child is a responsibility. But, more so than that, it is a privilege and a great blessing. It is indeed, a gift from God. God blesses us for a very short time with the gift and stewardship of a beautiful unique child to love and to form, and then to let go of ... so that child may fulfill the mission God intended before that child even existed. We as parents, are part of that great mystery and that mission. Our prayer is that we, and all parents, will faithfully fulfill our part for the greater glory of God. We are confident that we can do just that, if and only if we remain united to him. God bless you, and *God love you*!

In the name of the Father, and of the Son, and of the Holy Spirit. Amen.

THE END

Epilogue

For he is our peace.
(Ephesians 2:14)

We hope that the reader will have benefited in some manner from what we have shared. If there is anything good in this book please give worship and glory to the Holy Spirit; anything bad or detrimental, responsibility belongs to us. "Neither the planter nor the waterer matters, only God, who makes things grow." (1 Corinthians 3:7)

Please count on the prayers of the Littleton family for each of you. You are always included in each of our Masses, Eucharistic visits, rosaries, prayers, sacrifices, and crosses. Though we do not know most of you by name, God knows who you are, and will honor our meager intercession for you. *Could you pray for us too?*

We place the fruits of this book first and foremost into the trustworthy hands of the Blessed Virgin Mary. It was through her intercession, through no merit of our own, that our family received the sublime <u>gift</u> of a deep and active faith in Jesus Christ, our Lord.

We conclude with a few words of encouragement from the heart, which we find best expressed through the word of God:

"No need to recall the past, no need to think about what was done before. See, I am doing a new deed, even now it comes to light; can you not see it?" (Isaiah 43:18-19)

"For I, Yahweh, your God, I am holding you by the right hand; I tell you, 'do not be afraid, I will help you.'" (Isaiah 41:13)

"I have said these things to you while still with you; but the Advocate, the Holy Spirit whom the Father will send in my name, will teach you everything and remind you of all that I have said to you. Peace I bequeath to you, my own peace I give you, a peace the world cannot give, this is my gift to you. Do not let your hearts be troubled or afraid." (John 14:25-27)

"I want you to be happy, always happy in the Lord; I repeat what I want is your happiness. Let your tolerance be evident to everyone; the Lord is very near.

EPILOGUE

There is no need to worry; but if there is anything you need, pray for it, asking God for it with prayer and thanksgiving, and that peace of God, which is so much greater than we can understand, will guard your hearts and your thoughts in Christ Jesus. Finally, brothers, fill your minds with everything that is true, everything that is noble, everything that is good and pure, everything that we love and honor, and everything that can be thought virtuous and worthy of praise." (Philippians 4:4-8)

"Do not be afraid; only have faith."
(Mark 5:37)

"May Yahweh bless you and keep you. May Yahweh let his face shine on you and be gracious to you. May Yahweh uncover his face to you and bring you peace." (Numbers 6:24-26)

Abbreviations and Resources

To make the reading and reference process as convenient as possible for the reader we are abbreviating the following:

CCC: *Catechism of the Catholic Church Second Edition* (Excerpts from the English translation of the *Catechism of the Catholic Church* for the United States of America copyright 1994, United States Catholic Conference, Inc.-Libreria Editrice Vaticana) English translation of the Catechism of the Catholic Church: Modifications from the Editio Typica copyright 1997, United States Catholic Conference, Inc.-Libreria Editrice Vaticana. Used with Permission.

TCM: *The Ten Commandments of Matrimony*, author unknown

Diary St. Maria Faustina Kowalska: *Divine Mercy in My Soul* © 1987 Congregation of Marians of the Immaculate Conception, Stockbridge, MA 01263. Used with permission.

Sheen, Fulton J., *Life of Christ*: Copyright © 1958, 1977 Foreword copyright © 1990 by Doubleday, a division of Random House, Inc.

Sheen, Fulton J., *Your Life is Worth Living: The Christian Philosophy of Life*, Copyright © 2001 by Jon Hallingstad; Published by St. Andrew's Press.

Familiaris Consortio, Pope John Paul II

http://www.vatican.va/holy_father/john_paul_ii/apost_exhortations/documents/hf_jp-ii_exh_19811122_familiaris-consortio_en.html

Gaudium et Spes, Pope Paul VI

http://www.vatican.va/archive/hist_councils/ii_vatican_council/documents/vat-ii_cons_19651207_gaudium-et-spes_en.html

Letter to Families, Pope John Paul II

http://www.vatican.va/holy_father/john_paul_ii/letters/documents/hf_jp-ii_let_02021994_families_en.html

The Truth and Meaning of Human Sexuality, Pontifical Council for the Family

http://www.vatican.va/roman_curia/pontifical_councils/family/documents/rc_pc_family_doc_08121995_human-sexuality_en.html

About the Authors

Jim and Kathleen Littleton have been married for twenty-three years and live in the Chicago metropolitan area. They are the parents of nineteen children, fourteen living on earth and five living in heaven. Kathleen is an attorney by profession and holds an undergraduate degree in secondary education. She put her career aside when her first child was born to raise her family. Jim works fulltime in Catholic ministry and owns two small businesses. Both are actively involved in the ministry of faith formation and evangelization. They are available as a couple or individually as speakers.

Those interested in contacting Jim and/or Kathleen Littleton about speaking engagements can email them at **Jimandkathleen@aol.com**

LaVergne, TN USA
09 May 2010
182076LV00001B/13/P